NORTH KOREA

A CLOSER LOOK AT THE SECRET STATE

By Eleanor Bradshaw

LUCENT
PRESS

Published in 2020 by
Lucent Press, an Imprint of Greenhaven Publishing, LLC
353 3rd Avenue
Suite 255
New York, NY 10010

Designer: Deanna Paternostro
Editor: Diane Bailey

Library of Congress Cataloging-in-Publication Data

Names: Bradshaw, Eleanor, author.
Title: North Korea : a closer look at the secret state / Eleanor Bradshaw.
Description: New York : Lucent Press, [2020] | Series: World history |
  Includes bibliographical references and index.
Identifiers: LCCN 2019003954 (print) | LCCN 2019004087 (ebook) | ISBN
  9781534567900 (eBook) | ISBN 9781534567894 (pbk.) | ISBN 9781534567177
  (library bound)
Subjects: LCSH: Korea (North)–History. | Korea (North)–Politics and
  government.
Classification: LCC DS935 (ebook) | LCC DS935 .B73 2020 (print) | DDC
  951.93–dc23
LC record available at https://lccn.loc.gov/2019003954

Printed in the United States of America

CPSIA compliance information: Batch #BS19KL: For further information contact Greenhaven Publishing LLC, New York, New York at 1-844-317-7404.

Please visit our website, www.greenhavenpublishing.com. For a free color catalog of all our high-quality books, call toll free 1-844-317-7404 or fax 1-844-317-7405.

Contents

Foreword — 4

Setting the Scene: A Timeline — 6

Introduction:
The Secret State — 8

Chapter One:
Kingdoms and Dynasties — 13

Chapter Two:
The World at War — 30

Chapter Three:
The Korean War — 43

Chapter Four:
A Family of Leaders — 57

Chapter Five:
Making Headlines — 77

Epilogue:
Who Are North Koreans? — 91

Notes — 95

For More Information — 98

Index — 100

Picture Credits — 103

About the Author — 104

Foreword

History books are often filled with names and dates—words and numbers for students to memorize for a test and forget once they move on to another class. However, what history books should be filled with are great stories, because the history of our world is filled with great stories. Love, death, violence, heroism, and betrayal are not just themes found in novels and movie scripts. They are often the driving forces behind major historical events.

When told in a compelling way, fact is often far more interesting—and sometimes far more unbelievable—than fiction. World history is filled with more drama than the best television shows, and all of it really happened. As readers discover the incredible truth behind the triumphs and tragedies that have impacted the world since ancient times, they also come to understand that everything is connected. Historical events do not exist in a vacuum. The stories that shaped world history continue to shape the present and will undoubtedly shape the future.

The titles in this series aim to provide readers with a comprehensive understanding of pivotal events in world history. They are written with a focus on providing readers with multiple perspectives to help them develop an appreciation for the complexity of the study of history. There is no set lens through which history must be viewed, and these titles encourage readers to analyze different viewpoints to understand why a historical figure acted the way they did or why a contemporary scholar wrote what they did about a historical event. In this way, readers are able to sharpen their critical-thinking skills and apply those skills in their history classes. Readers are aided in this pursuit by formally documented quotations and annotated bibliographies, which encourage further research and debate.

Many of these quotations come from carefully selected primary sources, including diaries, public records, and contemporary research and writings. These valuable primary sources help readers hear the voices of those who directly experienced historical events, as well as the voices of biographers and historians who provide a unique perspective on familiar topics. Their voices all help history come alive in a vibrant way.

As students read the titles in this series, they are provided with clear context in the form of maps, timelines, and informative text. These elements give them the basic facts they need to fully appreciate the high drama that is history.

The study of history is difficult at times—not because of all the information that needs to be memorized, but because of the challenging questions it asks us. How could something as horrible as the Holocaust happen? What are the roots of the struggle for peace in the Middle East? Why are some people reluctant to call themselves feminists? The information presented in each title gives readers the tools they need to confront these questions and participate in the debates they inspire.

As we pore over the stories of events and eras that changed the world, we come to understand a simple truth: No one can escape being a part of history. We are not bystanders; we are active participants in the stories that are being created now and will be written about in history books decades and even centuries from now. The titles in this series help readers gain a deeper appreciation for history and a stronger understanding of the connection between the stories of the past and the stories they are part of right now.

SETTING THE SCENE: A TIMELINE

2333 BC ····· 57 BC ···· AD 668 ···· 918 ····· 1392 ····· 1910 ····· 1919 ····· 1945 ·······

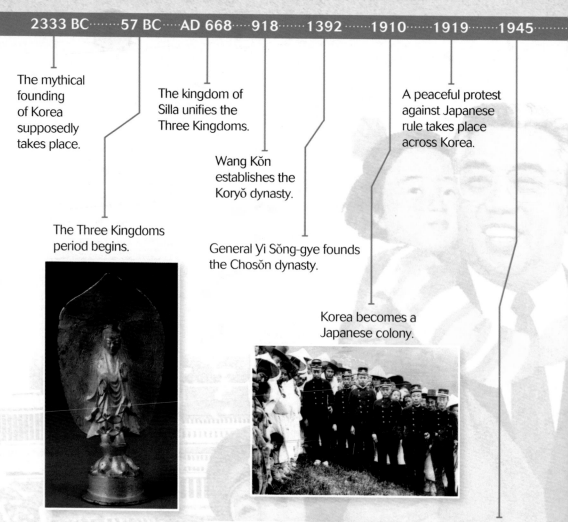

The mythical founding of Korea supposedly takes place.

The kingdom of Silla unifies the Three Kingdoms.

A peaceful protest against Japanese rule takes place across Korea.

Wang Kŏn establishes the Koryŏ dynasty.

The Three Kingdoms period begins.

General Yi Sŏng-gye founds the Chosŏn dynasty.

Korea becomes a Japanese colony.

Korea is divided along the 38th parallel.

Kim Jong Il dies; Kim Jong-Un takes power.

The Democratic People's Republic of Korea is established.

The Korean War comes to an end with an armistice.

The Korean War begins with a surprise attack.

Kim Il-Sung dies and is succeeded by Kim Jong Il.

North Korea successfully tests an intercontinental ballistic missile.

THE SECRET STATE

The Korean peninsula has been home to clans, tribes, kingdoms, and dynasties throughout its long history. Each civilization has left its mark, dividing the land into puzzle pieces that have changed over time, echoing the natural contours of the mountain ranges, river valleys, and coastal plains that compose the Korean landscape.

Land of Silver and Gold

The most recent division in Korea's history occurred in 1945 with the separation of North Korea from South Korea. Despite their centuries of shared history, the two areas developed in distinctly different ways from this point on. In 1948, the Democratic People's Republic of Korea (DPRK) was formed in the north, although the country is commonly known simply as North Korea. The country is also called Chosŏn by its people, a name that reflects a rich heritage and identification with the peninsula's early history.

"Let morning shine on this land of silver and gold,"[1] North Korea's national anthem begins. The song goes on to praise the country's natural features, abundant resources, strong and dedicated people, and long history. In the last century, that history has been steeped in conflicts that have tested and shaped the country's spirit.

The Hermit Kingdom

Today, North Korea is a state that is almost completely cut off from the global community. This insular position is not new to the peninsula, which has historically reacted to outside invasions with withdrawal and isolationism. In the 1800s, the whole of Korea became known as the "Hermit Kingdom" as a result of its disinterest in foreign affairs and resistance to outside influences. Although the peninsula shares this history of isolation, South Korea has since become a participant in world affairs and culture while North Korea continues

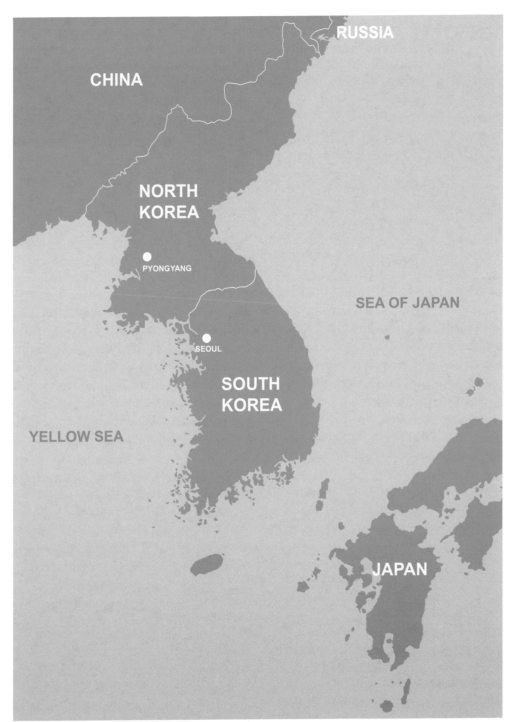

North Korea shares borders with China and Russia to the north. The capital of North Korea is commonly written as Pyongyang or P'yŏngyang.

to remain aloof, taking a fierce pride in its homogeneous national culture and self-sufficiency.

Before the Korean War of the 1950s permanently divided the peninsula into North and South Korea, Korean identity was strengthened and tested through various periods of foreign domination. China made repeated forays into Korea from ancient times to the modern era. Mongolia invaded and occupied parts of Korea in both the 11th and 13th centuries. In the 19th and 20th centuries, Japan and Russia also entered the Korean peninsula and attempted to shape and direct its fate. Even during these periods of invasion and occupation, Koreans managed to maintain their own national character, borrowing features from other cultures and reshaping them to suit their own needs and creative tastes.

After weathering the oppression of the Japanese occupation from 1910 to 1945, North Korea faced yet another challenge. World War II had brought an end to the Japanese occupation, but it introduced a new conflict that divided the peninsula in half and pitted the two sides against each other. The Soviet Union and China supported the North, while the United States championed the South. The fighting of the Korean War lasted for three years, from 1950 to 1953, but its long-term impacts reverberate across the entire peninsula today.

Known in North Korea as the Fatherland Liberation War, the Korean War resulted in widespread destruction and heavy casualties on all sides. The cities of the North were annihilated by aggressive bombing campaigns led by the United States. The crimes and tragedies of the war may have faded in American memory, but North Koreans distinctly remember the devastation of their country. This history motivates the extremely protective stance North Korea has maintained over its people, assets, and military capabilities since the war.

A Communist Monarchy

Following the war, North Korea launched into a period of nation-building under the guidance of the Soviet Union and China. These Communist countries promoted a way of living in which all property is owned and distributed by the state. In this model, citizens work for the state and in return receive what they need—such as food and housing—from the government. As a result, communist ideology shaped the governmental structure and policies of North Korea as a fledgling country.

North Korea's economy and infrastructure rapidly advanced under its Communist allies and the watchful eye of its first leader, Kim Il-Sung. Cities were rebuilt, electricity restored, farms replanted, and factories established. The transformation of North Korea from a charred battleground to a thriving country in these early years earned Kim Il-Sung the loyalty of the North Korean people. National success,

Anti-American propaganda is a common sight in the cities, schools, and public art of North Korea. The United States has traditionally been seen as the great enemy of the North Korean people.

combined with heavy propaganda and the suppression of opposition, helped to create an almost godlike status for Kim Il-Sung. Even today, his larger-than-life persona is still a vital part of North Korean culture.

When Kim Il-Sung died in 1994, power passed to his son, Kim Jong Il. Although the North Korean economy was stagnating by this point, Kim Jong Il inherited a measure of his father's mythical standing. The current leader, Kim Jong-Un, who came to power in 2011, represents the third generation of what is sometimes called the world's only communist monarchy, which is based in the perceived superiority of the Kim family. All three members of the Kim dynasty have ruthlessly stamped out opposition, taken an antagonistic stance toward other nations, and maintained a tight grip on the country's people and its nearly impenetrable borders. Very little is known about ordinary North Korean people besides the information shared by defectors, people who have escaped and permanently left behind their lives in what has become known as the secret state.

In the 1990s, the Soviet Union collapsed, and North Korea lost the steady support from its Communist allies that had kept it afloat since the Korean War. The resulting economic struggles and stagnation caused North Korean development to falter. Famines, floods, and poorly managed resources resulted in widespread poverty and hunger in North Korea. These problems challenged the communist ideology of North Korea and forced it, in recent years, to introduce free-market practices to stimulate economic growth. Moving forward, this crack in the country's communist armor may open the door to a new and different way of life in North Korea.

CHAPTER ONE

KINGDOMS AND DYNASTIES

Until 1945, North and South Korea shared a common history. From the earliest Stone Age settlers, the people of Korea used the land's abundant natural resources to survive and thrive, eventually developing advanced kingdoms and dynasties.

The first Paleolithic Korean settlers most likely came from Manchuria, an area in northeastern China, and Siberia, a vast region in northern Asia and modern-day Russia. In addition to traveling south, early Koreans may have crossed land bridges that once existed between the peninsula and Japan. These people survived along the coasts and river valleys by living in caves, gathering food, and making stone tools to aid in hunting and fishing.

After the last Ice Age ended almost 12,000 years ago, rising sea levels closed the land bridges with Japan. The Neolithic era took shape as early humans learned to adapt to their new environment and was in full force in Korea by 3000 BC. During this period, Koreans were building small shelters, crafting pottery, making stone tools and blades, and constructing stone tombs. In addition to hunting and gathering, they also began to practice agriculture.

The next historic phase began around 1500 BC with the Korean Bronze Age. Archaeologists have unearthed pieces of jewelry, belt buckles, bells, swords, mirrors, and axes that Koreans made as they mastered bronze work. Many of these items have been found in burial tombs. Fine goods and rich metalwork in these tombs point to the development of a privileged and powerful group within the greater Korean society. At this point, social structures were changing, and it would not be long until the first recorded Korean state, Old Chosŏn, was established.

Old Chosŏn

Old Chosŏn, also known as Gojoseon, was the first known state established

KOREAN ARCHAEOLOGY

Archaeological sites and artifacts provide clues about life in ancient Korea. Through them, archaeologists are able to reconstruct the ways that Koreans connected with and borrowed from neighboring cultures and can trace the social and cultural development of the people of the peninsula.

Over 30,000 dolmens have been found in the Korean peninsula. These large stone structures are grave markers and are usually located above burial chambers. Items inside the burial chambers show the sophisticated social structures, ritual practices, and artistry prevalent among the ancient Koreans. Jewelry and other fine goods show the social importance and power of the deceased.

Some archaeological artifacts are found in former living spaces. Archaeological sites can tell historians how homes were arranged and built. Middens, or trash heaps, provide information about what early Koreans cooked and ate. Weapons offer insight into historic conflicts, and tools show the development of farming practices.

Pottery is another important archaeological find. It developed alongside agriculture as a way of storing and cooking food. Pottery allowed people to keep larger amounts of food for longer periods of time, giving them the food stability they needed in order to settle in one place and not be constantly moving in search of new sources of food. People used their fingernails, shells, sticks, and bones to decorate an early style of pottery known as Mumun pottery. It was replaced in the Bronze Age with a plainer style borrowed from Manchuria. Pottery styles continued to evolve throughout Korean history.

on the Korean peninsula. At the beginning of the Bronze Age, Koreans were living in clans, or extended family units. Their homes were dug into hillsides and clustered together in small groups. Old Chosŏn likely arose as a tribal state when alliances were forged between clans in northwestern Korea along the Taedong River.

Korean mythology tells a more colorful story about the founding of Old Chosŏn in 2333 BC. In Korean folklore, there was an age of gods. The creator god, Hwanin, allowed his son Hwanung to descend to Earth and live in an eastern land where the sun rose.

According to the legend, Hwanung established a divine city. He taught humans agriculture, medicine, and a variety of arts. The city was so pleasant that even wild animals were attracted to it. Hwanung helped a bear become

In Korea, dolmens are called koindol *or* chisongmyo. *This dolmen was constructed during the Bronze Age in Munhung-ri, not far from modern-day P'yŏngyang in North Korea.*

human so that she could live in the city. After her transformation, Hwanung married her. Their son Tangun became the first king of Chosŏn—"the land of morning calm."

There is little historic evidence to support Tangun's existence. However, the story of his life and kingdom are culturally important in both North and South Korea. Tangun is celebrated as the ancestor and unifier of the Korean people.

Although historians sometimes disagree over the definition of Old Chosŏn as a state, the period when it was founded was undoubtedly significant since the Iron Age coincided with its development. In addition to bronze tools and goods, Korean people now made iron plows and sickles for farming, as well as iron weapons and tools for warfare. They built wooden

North Koreans believe that Tangun was born on Mount Paektu, Korea's highest peak. Kim Jong Il was also reportedly born there. This popular mythology links the Kim leaders with the divine founding of Korea.

houses and developed *ondol*, a system of underfloor heating that redistributes heat from wood smoke, that is still used today.

In 194 BC, a man named Wiman became the ruler of Old Chosŏn. Some sources say that Wiman was Chinese, but he may have been a Chosŏn native. Either way, forces from China were coming closer to the Korean state, and by 108 BC, the Chinese Han Empire had taken control of Old Chosŏn and replaced it with four Chinese colonies.

The Three Kingdoms

As regional tribes and clans continued to form alliances with each other throughout the peninsula, three distinct states emerged. For the next 700 years, the three states fought off

SAMGUK YUSA AND THE STORY OF TANGUN

The *Samguk yusa* provides a history of Korea through folktales and legends and identifies Old Chosŏn as the first Korean state. Written in 1281 by a Buddhist monk named Iryeon, it gives the first historic record of the legendary founding of Korea:

> At that time a bear and a tiger were living in a cave. They prayed constantly to Hwanung to be turned into humans. At last he gave them a wick of wormwood and twenty garlic cloves and told them, "If you eat these and for one hundred days avoid the light of the sun, you will become human."

> The bear and tiger took them and ate. The bear, after twenty-one days of avoiding the sun, turned into a human, but the tiger could not avoid it and failed to become human. The bear that had become a human could not find a mate, and so by the holy altar tree prayed to become pregnant. Hwanung thereupon changed for a while into human form, and joined her in marriage. She became pregnant and gave birth to a son. He was named Tan'gun Wanggŏm.[1]

1. David McCann, *Early Korean Literature: Selections and Introductions*. New York, NY: Columbia University Press, 2000, p. 16.

foreign invasions and struggled with each other for land and supremacy. This stretch of Korean history is known as the Three Kingdoms period.

In 57 BC, Silla became the first kingdom to emerge. Koguryŏ followed in 37 BC, and Paekche was formed in 18 BC. Each of the three kingdoms saw the rise of aristocratic classes, the establishment of strict social hierarchies, and the centralization of power.

Common people worked for the state and had to pay high taxes. The three kingdoms developed separate and distinct cultures, but all three included the new influences of Buddhism and Confucianism from China. Buddhism was practiced across the peninsula and eventually became the official religion in each kingdom.

Modern-day North Koreans identify most strongly with the people of of the Koguryŏ legacy. Early tombs were built of stones, while later tombs were encased in mounds of earth. More than 10,000 Koguryŏ tombs still survive in North Korea and China, where workers built them for elite members of the royalty and aristocracy. Some of these tombs feature elaborately painted walls that show lively scenes and representations of the tomb's occupant and family members. This artwork offers unique insights into Koguryŏ culture. Tomb paintings depict how people looked and dressed, what their homes and villages looked like, and what things they valued during this era.

During the Three Kingdoms period, a fourth territory developed at the southern tip of the Korean peninsula when a group of small states banded together. Some believe the Kaya Confederacy was established in the year AD 42, but the real date is unknown. When the Silla Kingdom conquered Kaya in 562, it set into motion an expansion agenda that would eventually absorb the other kingdoms and unify the country.

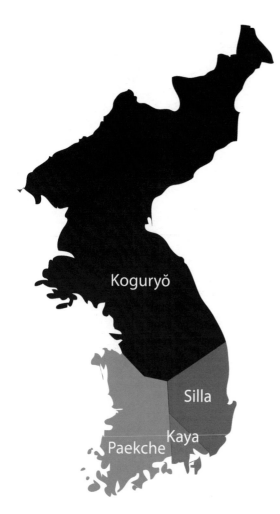

The Korean peninsula and parts of China were divided into three main kingdoms. The land that makes up North Korea today fell within the Koguryŏ Kingdom.

Koguryŏ. This kingdom's territory covered a large northern section of the peninsula and reached up into areas of Manchuria in China, which influenced Koguryŏ's cultural development.

Ancient tombs are an important part

Unified Silla

With the help of the Chinese Tang dynasty, Silla conquered the kingdoms of Paekche in 660 and Koguryŏ in 668. By 676, it had also driven the Chinese out of Korea. This is commonly considered the first time that most of the Korean peninsula was united under one kingdom and one central monarch. The name Unified Silla reflects the political unity that characterized this period.

This tomb painting is located near modern-day P'yŏngyang. In it, a large pot of rice cooks as individuals work in a kitchen. Nearby, images of carriage sheds and meat hung up to dry provide further details about daily life in Koguryŏ.

In North Korea, however, historians generally view Koguryŏ as the country's first unified kingdom. Even after Silla's conquests, some Koguryŏ people remained independent. They lived near the Yalu River in the border area between modern-day Korea, China, and Russia, which became known as Parhae. In 721, Silla built a wall to protect against invasions from the north and reinforce the boundaries between Parhae and Unified Silla. The present-day separation of North and South Korea is an echo of this historic division.

Unified Silla was a wealthy state with agricultural and manufactured goods to trade, as well as vibrant scientific, artistic, scholarly, and cultural activity. Silla's ancient capital in Kyŏngju was known as the "city of gold." It became a hub of sophisticated culture and advanced pursuits in math, astronomy, history, and education.

Although the Silla Kingdom was politically independent from China, Chinese culture and trade continued to influence the development of Korean culture. Confucianism and Buddhism had been important during the Three Kingdoms period, and they became dominant forces in shaping the structure and achievements of Unified Silla. Monks and students traveled to and from China, bringing back cultural knowledge and incorporating it into Korean life.

Chinese Confucianism provided Silla with a model of good government. Its political philosophy helped establish a framework for government structures and systems in Unified Silla. Confucianism can be described as a worldview that values respect for ancestors, the importance of education, merit-based advancement, and the systematic organization of society and government. The civil service examination is a Confucian creation that became prominent in Korea during the Unified Silla period. Civil service exams were meant to identify and place qualified people in governmental positions by testing their knowledge. In theory, this would open up powerful positions to individuals outside the aristocracy. The National Confucian Academy was established in 682 for instructing government officials, and civil service exams for statesmen began in 788.

Despite the democratic appeal of Confucianism, the rulers of ancient Silla belonged exclusively to the aristocracy. The rigid social hierarchy of Silla was based on "bone rank." This hereditary system of class structure divided Koreans into fixed groups. It determined the rights and responsibilities of different members of society and secured political power for a select group. Only high-ranking members of society were allowed to take the civil service exams, limiting the pool of leaders to members of the aristocracy.

If Confucianism provided a political framework for Unified Silla, Buddhism provided a religious one. Buddhism offered a rich spiritual life to its followers,

The Bell of King Sŏngdŏk is an impressive example of Unified Silla craftsmanship. This bronze bell, weighing nearly 21 tons (19 mt), was created in 771 and adorned with Buddhist figures and Chinese characters.

THE GREAT DHARANI SUTRA

Among Buddhist monks, it was common practice to copy religious teachings for followers to read. The invention of woodblock printing around the year 660 made this job easier. With this technique, an image or text is carved into wood, spread with ink, and then pressed onto paper. This allows multiple copies to be made. Although the practice developed in China, the oldest-known example of woodblock printing was found in Korea in 1966. At that time, as workers restored a stone pagoda at the Bulguksa Temple in South Korea, they uncovered a printed document that had been hidden from view for 1,300 years. Scholars date the creation of the document to between 700 and 751, during the Unified Silla period. It is the oldest printed document in the world.

Known as *The Great Dharani Sutra of Immaculate and Pure Light*, the scroll uses Chinese characters on a traditional Korean paper called *hanji*. It tells the story of the Buddha saving a man's life. The discovery is an example of the way Chinese practices, such as Buddhism and woodblock printing, were incorporated into Korean cultural achievements during the Unified Silla period.

Buddhist scriptures are engraved on this collection of woodblocks created in the 13th century. Woodblock printing allowed Buddhist monks to more effectively spread Buddhist scripture.

influencing not only religious practices but also art, architecture, literature, and daily life. Stone and metal religious art, such as large bronze bells and gilded sculptures, reflected Buddhist themes. Many architectural masterpieces of Buddhist tombs, temples, and stone pagodas still stand in Korea today. In addition, Buddhist texts used advanced printmaking techniques and formed an important body of literature.

A great deal changed in 935 when the last king of Unified Silla surrendered his power. The state had been in decline for more than a century as nobles fought with each other and destabilized the authority and effectiveness of the government. This elite group at the top of the social hierarchy, the "true bone," created their own armies and engaged in internal squabbles. The peasant classes also revolted to protest heavy taxes, leading to a deeply unstable kingdom.

The old states of the Three Kingdoms period began to rise up against Silla. A leader from the north,

Wang Kŏn, was friends with the faltering Silla king, and this relationship gave him the advantage he needed to gain power. After a peaceful transfer of power, Wang Kŏn led Korea out of the increasingly unstable Unified Silla period and into the Koryŏ dynasty.

The Koryŏ Dynasty

As Unified Silla waned, Wang Kŏn had seized power in his home kingdom of Later Koguryŏ in 918. From there, he secured control of Silla in 935. When

Later Paekche surrendered in 936, Wang Kŏn succeeded in uniting the kingdoms of the Korean peninsula into a truly single nation for the first time. Seeking cultural unification as well, Wang Kŏn married a Silla princess and welcomed members of previous states. After his death, Wang Kŏn became known as the "Great Founder." The country he unified was called Koryŏ, which inspired the Western name Korea.

Until its fall in 1392, the Koryŏ dynasty witnessed the ebb and flow of many of the cultural, political, and religious traditions that were hallmarks of the Three Kingdoms and Unified Silla. China remained an important partner in economic and cultural exchanges. Buddhism and Confucianism continued to thrive, as did art and literature.

Celadon pottery is one of the greatest lasting artistic contributions from the Koryŏ dynasty. The term celadon refers to ceramics with a greenish-blue, translucent glaze. Celadon originally developed in China, but skilled Koryŏ potters took it to new heights, creating highly prized pieces with organic forms and inlaid designs. These functional works of art were traded with China and other countries.

Buddhism also continued to inspire splendid artistic achievements.

Many Koryŏ potters used Buddhist motifs, such as the lotus flower details featured on the base of this cup. Koryŏ celadon can be found in many museums today.

Buddhist temples featured giant Buddhas sculpted from boulders, as well as gilded figures and illuminated manuscripts. During the Koryŏ period, Buddhist monks created the *Tripitaka Koreana*, the world's largest and oldest collection of Buddhist scripture. The first set of woodblocks they used, from the 11th century, were lost after a Mongol invasion, but Buddhist monks completed their mission for a second time in 1251, engraving more than 80,000 woodblocks over a 16-year period. About 6,000 volumes were printed from the woodblocks. The original woodblocks survive and are housed as a national treasure in South Korea.

In addition to advances in woodblock printing, Koryŏ innovators developed a new form of printmaking. Gutenberg's printing press, a German invention from 1450, is generally celebrated for revolutionizing the world of printing. More than 200 years earlier, however, printers in Koryŏ had already developed the first system of metal movable type. *Jikji*, a Koryŏ volume of Buddhist scriptures from 1377, is the oldest existing book printed this way.

Literature from the Koryŏ period

Koryŏ printers cast these Chinese characters in bronze. During the printing process, the characters would have been lined up between strips of bamboo, covered with ink, and pressed against paper.

extends beyond Buddhist texts to include national histories, prose, and poetry. Historians were working during this time to record the lengthy past of the Korean peninsula. Both the *Samguk sagi* from 1146 and the *Samguk yusa* from 1285 include ancient tales, legends, and biographies. The *Samguk sagi* is known in English as the "Historical Record of the Three Kingdoms."

Such artistic and literary achievements occurred in a political and social climate that saw advancements and struggles that were similar to those of previous dynasties. Power was concentrated in the hands of a few, and there was discontent among those who lacked power, social status, and economic opportunity.

Just as it had done in Unified Silla, Confucianism found a stronghold in the Koryŏ dynasty, with Confucian schools and principles shaping the government. The *Samguk sagi* promoted Confucian ideals of merit and opportunity, especially in the story of Nokchin, an advisor to the king. In the text, Nokchin points out the negative effects of arbitrarily giving power to people who are not qualified to use it wisely. He recommends a Confucian approach—one that matches abilities with responsibilities—to filling administrative positions:

If you place men of great talent in high positions and men of lesser talent in low positions, then from the six ministers and one hundred officials at court down to provincial governors and local magistrates, no position will be unfilled and none will be occupied by an unqualified person. There will be then perfect order high and low, and the wise and the incompetent will be kept apart. Only then will you achieve a royal rule.[2]

A rigid social structure still existed. The top tier of government officials controlled Koryŏ land and determined the direction and structure of the government. They orchestrated the lives of those below them, including merchants and peasants who worked the land. An outcast class of tradesmen, such as butchers and tanners, fell even lower on the social ladder. A class of slaves—about 30 percent of the population—came at the very bottom of Koryŏ society. Slavery was hereditary, offering no escape for those who were forced to work on the land and on government projects. As the Koryŏ dynasty progressed, more citizens called for the redistribution of land out of the hands of the elite.

The military also faced mistreatment as a result of the rigid social structure. In 1170, a political coup—the unlawful seizing of power—put a military regime in power for the next 60 years. Koryŏ history was spattered with uprisings and revolts by monks, the military, peasants, and slaves throughout the 12th century. By the time Mongols invaded in the 13th century, the political structure was weakened and vulnerable.

The Mongol leader Kublai Khan had already conquered China when his army invaded Korea in 1231. Over the next 30 years, several military campaigns resulted in deadly fighting with the Mongols. The Koryŏ government was eventually overthrown from within, and new civilian leaders organized a peace treaty with the Mongols in 1258. In the decades that followed, Mongols ruled and forced Koreans to help them in their failed campaigns to invade Japan.

When the Ming dynasty in China conquered the Mongols, Koreans had a chance to reclaim their land. General Yi Sŏng-gye took advantage of the disorder and chaos of the Koryŏ government and overthrew its leaders. In 1392, Yi Sŏng-gye ushered in the last and longest dynasty in Korean history, Chosŏn.

The Chosŏn Dynasty

General Yi Sŏng-gye chose the name of the first Korean state—Chosŏn—to replace the toppled Koryŏ dynasty, though the period is also known as the Yi dynasty. The general, a Confucian scholar and military leader, set out to reform Korea.

One of the major changes in Chosŏn was the fall of Buddhism. Buddhist institutions were destroyed as Confucianism was expanded and declared the new state religion. The state confiscated Buddhist temple lands, and Buddhist monks became outcasts in society. Neo-Confucianism broadened the principles of Confucianism to include an understanding and study of the universe, replacing the religious function that Buddhism had provided.

Neo-Confucianism also led to more widespread education through the growth of state-run schools. Members of a new, elite class of scholars called the *yangban* were assigned roles in the government and redistributed land among their group. Civil service examinations continued as a method for filling administrative roles, although they were limited to members of the yangban.

King Sejong, a notable figure within the Chosŏn dynasty, reigned from 1419 to 1450. During his rule, Korean culture flourished. There were intellectual advances in astronomy, science, and math, and a royal academy called Chiphyŏnjŏn, or the Hall of Worthies, was founded to conduct research in various areas. King Sejong also employed scholars to invent a writing system for the Korean language, and it was proclaimed the official language in 1446. Known as Hangul in South Korea and *Chosŏn muntcha* in North Korea, the alphabet now contains 10 vowels and 14 consonants. Before this point, Koreans had no written system of their own to record the Korean language and used Chinese characters instead. The invention of the Hangul alphabet allowed literature to be written in the Korean language for the first time. King Sejong hoped that his new system would make reading and writing more accessible to common people.

Admiral Yi Sun-shin's "turtle ships" were specially engineered for battle. Iron building materials helped protect sailors, spikes prevented the enemy from boarding the ship, and advanced weapons were used for attacks.

Though Chosŏn lasted longer than any other dynasty in Korean history, it was not without its challenges. The dynasty dealt with intermittent invasions from its neighbors, such as one in 1592 from Japanese troops. The incredible Chosŏn naval forces, led by Admiral Yi Sun-shin, fought them off with help from the Chinese. In 1597, another Japanese invasion was rebutted, but only after the attacking troops had destroyed palaces, homes, and national treasures throughout Korea. In the 1600s, Chosŏn once again faced attacks, this time from Manchu warriors from China. The Manchu tribes eventually took control of the Chinese Ming dynasty.

By the 1700s, Chosŏn had found its footing again. New irrigation methods improved the country's agriculture. A new school of practical learning called Silhak also found popularity. Silhak was a revolutionary philosophy that was critical of Neo-Confucianism. Silhak scholars studied and promoted practical efforts to reform agriculture, education, technology, and class structure. Western ideas also found their way into the country in the form of Roman Catholicism, which was introduced by European merchants and priests. With its teachings about equality and life after death, Roman Catholicism appealed to some members of the Silhak school and the peasant classes.

Although Roman Catholicism was welcomed by some citizens, the government viewed its ideology as dangerously contradictory to Neo-Confucianism. The government tried to suppress Catholicism by persecuting local converts and executing foreign priests and missionaries. Foreign merchants and diplomats also were excluded from Korean society.

In the 19th century, Chosŏn adopted a strict policy of isolation. It rebuffed offers of trade from foreign nations, including the United States, France, and Japan. The leaders of Chosŏn utilized violent means to send a clear message: They were willing to attack, burn, and sink merchant ships to let foreign nations know they were not interested in trade. This position earned Chosŏn the name "Hermit Kingdom." However, Japanese forces were at work to bring an end to the Chosŏn dynasty. By the late 19th century, the Korean peninsula found itself being pried open. Its resistance and desire for seclusion were not enough to overcome the wishes— and military might—of the rest of the world.

CHAPTER TWO

THE WORLD AT WAR

Despite the Chosŏn dynasty's efforts to isolate the Korean peninsula from international affairs, the world was pressing ever closer. China, Russia, and Japan all envied its geographic location. It became clear that the Chosŏn rule would not survive on its own, and by the 1880s, under King Kojong, Chosŏn officials began signing trade and diplomatic treaties to align Korea with various foreign nations.

In 1882, China engineered a treaty of commerce between the United States and Korea. Similar treaties with the United Kingdom, Germany, Russia, and France followed. However, these new connections threatened rather than preserved Korean independence. Japan's growing political and military powers were fixed on the Korean peninsula and the easy access it could offer to China and Russia. Global changes were brewing, and Korea found itself in the middle of international conflict.

Sino-Japanese War

As a country now open to foreign trade, Korea struggled with a new set of problems that divided the country. Some viewed modernization as the only way to keep up with Korea's new trading partners. Meanwhile, conservatives wanted to return to isolationism. The increased presence of representatives from foreign governments further complicated these debates.

Korea had long been a tributary state of China, meaning it was officially separate from China but still showed submission to its more powerful neighbor in return for protection. However, a skirmish with the Japanese had led the Chosŏn dynasty to sign the Treaty of Ganghwa with Japan in 1876. This treaty declared Korea an independent nation and loosened its bond to China.

Japan's interest in Korea was based partly on the peninsula's strategic position between Japan, China, and Russia. Access to Korea would grant Japan a wider reach into these northern countries. Japan also wished to open Korea for trade and mine its deposits of iron and coal. Japan's ambitions for Korea, however, placed the country squarely against China.

Tensions between Japan and China were running high when the Tonghak Uprising broke out in 1894. It was led by students and peasants who rejected the social inequality in Korea. When the Korean government asked China for help to suppress the rebellion, Japan also sent troops to intervene. Japan viewed the Chinese presence as a violation of current treaties. Although the Korean rebels surrendered, the two rival armies were left to face

Although Korea remained neutral when the Sino-Japanese War between Japan and China was declared, they were pressured to ally themselves with the Japanese shortly after. Here, Korean soldiers are seen with captured Chinese troops.

This is believed to be a photo of the Chosŏn dynasty's Empress Myeongseong, informally known as Queen Min, the wife of King—and then Emperor—Kojong. Her ties to China threatened Japan's interests in Korea, and Japanese assassins killed her in 1895.

each other on Korean soil. This incident sparked war between China and Japan.

From August 1, 1894, until April 17, 1895, the Sino-Japanese War raged between China and Japan. Once war was underway, Japanese forces took control of the Korean government and installed pro-Japanese administrators. The new Korean officials signed an alliance with Japan and provided food, supplies, and military support to help Japan drive the Chinese from Korea. After land and sea battles throughout Korea and China, Japan's more modern and superior military won. The Treaty of Shimonoseki ended the war, forcing China to surrender its hold on Korea. Japan's new influence and power allowed the country to direct Korean reforms and political changes for the rest of the century.

Some viewed Korea's break with China as positive and believed that the changes the Japanese brought to Korea were signs of progress. Others mourned for a time when Korea had more control over its own destiny rather than being pushed and pulled by foreign powers.

As Japan worked to transform Korea, Russia began encouraging Korean resistance to Japanese powers, seeking opportunity in Korea for itself. Russia had also secretly signed an alliance with China in 1896, pitting itself against Japan. Then, in 1897, King Kojong declared Korea to be an independent empire, cutting off ties to China. The stage was set for another war over Korea.

Russo-Japanese War

Russia and Japan had been eyeing each other across the Korean peninsula since the Sino-Japanese War. After the war, Russia and other European powers forced Japan to relinquish its hold on the Liaodong Peninsula in Manchuria. Japan was unhappy with this development and resented the growing presence of Russian troops in the area it had been forced to surrender. When Russia failed to honor its agreement to withdraw troops from Manchuria, Japan attacked. The Russo-Japanese War began on February 8, 1904, as Japan and Russia battled over their rights to parts of Manchuria and access to Korea.

Again, Korea hoped to remain neutral throughout the conflict, but in the end, Japan persuaded the Korean government to grant Japanese troops access to Korean territory to prepare and launch attacks. Japan's military strength guaranteed another victory, and the war ended the following year.

Japanese and Russian delegates met at the Portsmouth Naval Shipyard in Kittery, Maine, to negotiate the terms of peace. U.S. president Theodore Roosevelt mediated, and the Treaty of Portsmouth was signed on September 5, 1905. The second article of the treaty reinforced Japan's authority in the Korean peninsula:

The Imperial Russian Government, acknowledging that Japan possesses in Korea paramount political, military and economical interests engages

Theodore Roosevelt (center) was awarded the Nobel Peace Prize for his mediating role in the Treaty of Portsmouth. He joined delegates from Russia (left) and Japan (right) in deciding Korea's fate.

neither to obstruct nor interfere with measures for guidance, protection and control which the Imperial Government of Japan may find necessary to take in Korea.[3]

By November 1905, Korea had been bullied into becoming a Japanese protectorate. With no independent political control, the country was forced to rely on Japan. Korea's Emperor Kojong secretly appealed to the 1907 International Peace Conference in the Netherlands to intercede. Unfortunately, Korean delegates were denied admittance to the conference, and the effort had little effect beyond Emperor Kojong's forced abdication that year. His son Sunjong became the final ruler of Chosŏn.

In addition to the emperor's struggle against Japan, Korean guerrilla armies, known as "Righteous Armies," also rose up. These grassroots resistance fighters consisted mainly of Confucian scholars, Korean soldiers, and former officials who resented Japan's new power. They, too, could not prevent the rise of Japan, and Korea became a Japanese colony on August 22, 1910. On that day, Emperor Sunjong surrendered control and ended the 500-year Chosŏn period.

Japanese Occupation

A 35-year period of occupation followed Japan's annexation of Korea, bringing mixed results for the Korean people. In some ways, Japan made significant strides in modernizing Korea. However, these advances were offset by harsh treatment of the Korean people at the hands of the Japanese. Even today, the oldest generation of Koreans still remembers these abuses.

Japanese colonization was focused on the growth and development of Korean resources and infrastructure. Cities were rapidly renewed and expanded. Commerce grew, and new textile, steel, and chemical industries developed across the peninsula. Workers constructed railroads, highways, and ports. Elements of mass consumer culture, including radio and film, spread through the country. Although these efforts benefited Koreans in some ways, the primary goal of these developments was to advance Japanese people and interests. Koreans, who were under harsh Japanese military control, paid a high price for this progress.

On the heels of World War I, U.S. president Woodrow Wilson delivered a powerful speech with a blueprint for world peace. Wilson's statement, known as the "Fourteen Points," called for national self-determination. The idea was that the people of a nation—a group with a shared language, history, and culture—have the right to decide who governs them.

This call had special meaning in Korea, a clear and established nation that was under the control of a foreign country. When the deposed Emperor Kojong died in 1919, many Korean people were inspired to stand up against their unjust colonizers and endorse a Korean Declaration of Independence. Protests

THE TRAVELS OF ISABELLA BIRD BISHOP

An English traveler named Isabella Bird Bishop set out to explore Korea near the end of the Chosŏn dynasty, visiting four times between 1894 and 1897. In her book *Korea and Her Neighbors*, Bishop examined culture and politics in the changing climate of Korea. Korea was just beginning to open its borders to foreigners, and Bishop's observations provided one of the earliest firsthand accounts of Korea by a Westerner.

Bishop's view of Korea was colored by her identity as a British woman and a missionary. She saw the opening of Korea through trade agreements and the Sino-Japanese War as a sign of progress, and she praised the introduction of Western and Japanese practices to the region. In her book, she wrote,

> *The connection with China is at an end, and with the victories of Japan the Korean belief in the unconquerable military power of the Middle Kingdom has been exploded, and the alliance between two political systems essentially corrupt has been severed. The distinction between patrician and plebian has been abolished, on paper at least, along with domestic slavery ... Brutal punishments and torture are done away with, a convenient coinage has replaced cash, an improved educational system has been launched, a disciplined army and police force has been created, the Chinese literary examinations are no longer the test of fitness for official employment, a small measure of judicial reform has been granted, [and] a railroad from Chemulpo to the capital is being rapidly pushed to completion.*[1]

rippled across the nation beginning on March 1, 1919, and continued for several months. The Japanese brutally suppressed these peaceful protesters by killing, injuring, and arresting thousands. One eyewitness remembered:

> *They came at us—started beating up the crowd. Everybody panicked. Some marchers jumped right over the railing to the tracks below. Others were speared by bayonets. Those soldiers on horseback rounded up people, tied them with ropes, then went after more. They beat them with the handle end of the horse whip.*[4]

Despite Wilson's call for democracy and peace, the Western world failed to support Koreans in their independence movement. However, Japan loosened its grip slightly after the nationwide protest, and Koreans were granted more freedom. This relaxation in Japanese

In spite of her biases, her reflections and photographs provided a unique view into a country that had maintained its independence from the Western world for so much of its history.

1. Isabella Bird Bishop, *Korea and Her Neighbors: A Narrative of Travel, with an Account of the Vicissitudes and Position of the Country*, Volume 2. London, England: John Murray, 1898, pp. 283–284.

Isabella Bird Bishop, shown here in an image from about 1885, gave Western readers a glimpse into Korean life with her writings and photographs.

control did not last for long, however. World War II brought a renewed period of harsh controls and abuses as Japan forced Koreans to help them in their struggle against the Allies.

Many of the harshest measures inflicted on Koreans were intended to erase their culture and national identity. A Japanese elite class, for example, replaced the scholarly yangban. Confucianism was thrown out in favor of Japanese education, and Shintoism was pressed on the people as the accepted religion. Officials outlawed the Korean written language, Hangul. By 1939, more than 80 percent of Koreans had changed their names to Japanese names under pressure from their occupiers. Japanese hands rewrote Korean history, and thousands of historic artifacts were removed from Korea or destroyed.

Physical abuse added to the psychological effects of this cultural destruction. From 1937 to 1945, many Koreans

For many Koreans today, the wounds of Japanese occupation remain a source of pain and conflict. Many Korean women, such as the one whose picture is shown here, suffered devastating physical, sexual, and psychological abuse by the Japanese military.

were shipped out of their homeland to work in Japanese industries, fight on the front lines of the war, or labor on Japanese farms. Over 130,000 Koreans were taken to work 12 hours a day in Japanese mines under violent treatment and with little food or pay. In total, it is estimated that 3 million Koreans were sent abroad to assist with war efforts.

Among the victims of Japanese occupation were the so-called "comfort women." These young women—many of them still teenagers—were abducted by the Japanese or tricked into going to the front lines, where they were forced to serve the Japanese troops as sex workers. According to the United Nations (UN), 200,000 Korean women and girls suffered under this degrading institution of sexual slavery.

During this time of occupation, a group of resisters rose up to protect Korea and fight their oppressors. North Korea's future leader, Kim Il-Sung, was part of a group of Korean guerrilla fighters. He had joined the struggle in 1932, when Japan established another colony in Manchuria called Manchukuo. Kim and others fought back in the territory despite drastic Japanese measures that left only 200 guerrilla fighters alive by the end of World War II.

In August 1945, the Japanese surrendered to the Allied Forces. This brought an end to World War II and to the period of colonial control in Korea. By this

THE KOREAN INDEPENDENCE MOVEMENT

In *Under the Black Umbrella*, a collection of firsthand accounts of the Japanese occupation, a Korean named Kim Sunok recalled seeing waves of protesters arrive in the city of Seoul:

> One day when I was ten years old, I was playing near the tracks and I saw people in the tram. They wore Korean clothes but Western hats. Those hats—they took them off and waved them in the air, screaming at the top of their lungs, "Independence now!" I asked the grownups what was happening. They said they wanted to get their country back. Those people on the tram were going to Seoul to join a demonstration.
>
> A friend and I decided to follow. We went up the hill and down the other side toward Seoul. As we got near an area where noblemen of the Choson dynasty had their houses, we saw hundreds of Koreans, coming toward us shouting the same shout, "Independence now!"[1]

1. Quoted in Hildi Kang, *Under the Black Umbrella: Voices from Colonial Korea.* Ithaca, NY: Cornell University Press, 2001, pp. 17–18.

point, Korea had become highly industrialized and was second only to Japan as a modernized Asian country. Despite these technological advances, the country was still at the mercy of larger world powers that would once again decide Korea's fate.

Dividing Korea

Leaders of the Allied Forces had met at the Cairo Conference in 1943 to define their goals for resolving World War II. At the conference, U.S. president Franklin Roosevelt outlined a vision for the future of Asia, including Korea. The declaration released at this time stated that Korean independence was a goal for the Allies. In the words of the official press release, "Japan will also be expelled from all other territories which she has taken by violence and greed. The aforesaid three great powers [the United States, China, and Great Britain], mindful of the enslavement of the people of Korea, are determined that in due course Korea shall become free and independent."[5]

As World War II drew to a close, America prepared to do its part in achieving this goal. Despite Korea's long history of self-governance before the Japanese occupation, the United States believed it was necessary to intervene. Two American colonels looked at a map of Korea and drew an arbitrary line across the peninsula at the 38th parallel (a line of latitude located 38 degrees north of the equator). The land north of the line would fall under the guardianship of the Soviet Union, while the United States would take charge in the south.

One of the American colonels, Dean Rusk, recalled the race to divide Korea before the Soviet Union took control of the peninsula. In his memoir, *As I Saw It*, he recounted the hurried decision that would have a profound impact on Korea's future:

During a meeting on August 14, 1945, the same day as the Japanese surrender, [Bonesteel] and I retired to an adjacent room late at night and studied intently a map of the Korean peninsula. Working in haste and under great pressure, we had a formidable task: to pick a zone for the American occupation. Neither Tic nor I was a Korea expert, but it seemed to us that Seoul, the capital, should be in the American sector. We also knew that the U.S. Army opposed an extensive area of occupation. Using a National Geographic map, we looked just north of Seoul for a convenient dividing line but could not find a natural geographical line. We saw instead the thirty-eighth parallel and decided to recommend that.[6]

This was the first time in almost a millennium that the peninsula had been divided, although it was supposed to be a temporary solution. On September 8, 1945, less than a month after the Japanese fell, U.S. troops arrived in Korea. The Soviet Union had been present in the north since Japan's surrender. Thus, power in Korea was handed from the Japanese to two other foreign nations, once again bypassing Korea itself.

During World War II, the United States and Soviet Union had been wary allies, but after the war, they became increasingly hostile to one another. Although they did not engage in active fighting at this time, the period became known as the Cold War. This rivalry greatly influenced how the two countries managed their positions in Korea and extended its division from temporary to long-term, since both superpowers were equally reluctant to release their hold on Korea. The Communist Party took hold in the North, where the Soviet Union helped place Communist Koreans in positions of power. Kim Il-Sung returned to Korea from his guerrilla activities in China and made his first public appearance on October 14, 1945. He was quickly initiated into the new government structure as a national hero. These developments were deeply concerning to U.S. leaders who feared the spread of communism.

The Two Koreas

After failed attempts between the Soviet Union and the United States to begin reunifying Korea, the UN entered the ring. The UN planned to arrange an election in Korea, help establish the new government, and oversee the removal of the United States and Soviet Union. UN representatives arrived in Seoul in January 1948, but they were barred from entering North Korea. Elections went ahead in South Korea in May, and on August 15, 1948, the Republic of Korea was established under a new president, Syngman Rhee. This South Korean government emerged under the supervision of the UN, which recognized it as the only lawful government on the peninsula.

Meanwhile, a new government was forming in the North with the assistance of Soviet forces. In April 1948, a constitution had been proposed and accepted by an assembly of North Koreans. Elections were held in August. On September 9, 1948, the Democratic People's Republic of Korea (DPRK) was established with Kim Il-Sung as the state's premier (prime minister).

These two separate states met at the imaginary line of the 38th parallel. Both claimed to be the true state of the Korean peninsula, refusing to recognize each other as legitimate. With differing goals and politically charged alliances, both sides were poised for conflict.

CHAPTER THREE

THE KOREAN WAR

In the United States, the Korean War is also known as "the Forgotten War." Without a decisive victory or clear accomplishments, the war fought on distant Korean soil has seemed to fade in the collective memory of Americans. For Koreans, however, the war is far from forgotten.

The fighting lasted for three years, but the ramifications of the Korean War continue to reinforce the division of North and South Korea more than 60 years later. Complicated relationships with the United States exist on both sides of the divide. The Korean War was extraordinarily aggressive and destructive, a continuation of the peninsula's history of violence that began during the Japanese occupation. For all its bloodshed, it accomplished little more than to make both sides become more entrenched in their beliefs.

Reunifying Korea

After the creation of the North and South Korean governments, the occupying armies began their withdrawal. Soviet troops were gone by December 1948, leaving only military advisors behind. The United States followed suit, and by June 1949, the majority of American troops had also left the peninsula.

During this time, North Korea had been preparing to reclaim South Korea and reunify the entire peninsula. The Soviet Union had provided specialized military training for the Korean People's Army in the North. In addition to these well-trained troops, China had returned about 12,000 North Korean troops who had fought in the Chinese Civil War, a conflict that spanned more than two decades and ended in 1949 with the Communist Party taking control of China's government. The Soviet Union had also promised military equipment to North Korea. With a large, well-trained, and well-supplied army, North Korea was ready to begin its reunification strategy.

It is common to view the resulting conflict as an international war because of the involvement from the United States, China, and the Soviet Union. However, this struggle took place entirely on Korean soil and more closely resembled a civil war. In his book *The Korean War*, historian Bruce Cumings wrote, "Kim Il-Sung crossed the five-year-old 38th parallel, not an international boundary like that between Iraq and Kuwait, or Germany and Poland; instead it bisected a nation that had a rare and well-recognized unitary existence going back to antiquity."[7]

On June 25, 1950, fighting broke out between North and South Korean forces. Most accounts of the war say that North Korea initiated a surprise attack. However, North Korea insists that the South attacked first. Either way, it only took three days for North Korea's superior forces to advance and capture Seoul, South Korea's capital city.

The North's attack wiped out the majority of the South Korean troops. The country appealed to the United States for help, and President Harry Truman responded promptly. In addition to securing funding and American troops for South Korea, Truman also brought the matter to the United Nations. The UN officially condemned North Korea for attacking the South and authorized the use of peacekeeping forces on the peninsula. The United States and 16 other countries pledged to aid South Korea. The bulk of the UN forces came from the U.S. military, but units from the other countries were also involved.

The troops, led by General Douglas MacArthur, made a dramatic landing at Inch'ŏn Beach in South Korea. From there, they drove the North Korean forces back up to the 38th parallel. After a few days, Truman decided to order U.S. troops to advance farther, past the divide, with the goal of overthrowing the North Korean government. The UN soon approved this goal as well.

At this point, North Korea enlisted the support of China. The Communist leader Mao Zedong sent troops to join the struggle and tipped the balance in favor of North Korea. The Chinese and North Korean soldiers drove the fighting south of the 38th parallel once more. Another northward push from the UN forces brought the battle line back to where it had begun. After a few months of this tug-of-war, by the spring of 1951, the fighting had settled into a location slightly north of the 38th parallel, with both sides vigilantly holding the line.

American Airstrikes

To gain an advantage against North Korea, the U.S. military launched a devastating series of attacks from the air. Bombs and chemical weapons featured heavily in the U.S. airstrikes, with tragic results. Throughout the three-year war, American planes dropped 635,000 tons (576,062 mt) of bombs and chemical explosives on North Korea.

One of those chemical weapons was napalm, which was developed and used for the first time near the end of World War II. Napalm is a mixture of highly flammable fuel and gel that is specially designed to spray, spread, and burn whatever it hits. It is potent enough to set water on fire and melt human flesh. During the Korean War, the United States dropped 32,557 tons (29,535 mt) of napalm on North Korea.

B-29 planes were also used to drop bombs on specific targets, such as trains, bridges, factories, supply depots, and hydroelectric plants. The goal was to cut off supply lines used by North Korean troops and to stop Communist allies from China and the Soviet Union from entering the country.

American airstrikes were brutally efficient at destroying cities, which were particular targets at the start of the war. After North Korea's major cities had been leveled, B-29 missions shifted to destroying other resources. In May 1953, five dams in North Korea were bombed, causing flooding that ruined profitable farmland and rice supplies. China and Russia stepped in to help by sending food; without it, many North Koreans would have starved.

Near the end of the war, Truman began preparing for the possible use of atomic weapons, which the United States had launched against Japan during World War II. In the end, these weapons were not used, perhaps because previous explosives had already destroyed all of North Korea's large cities. By the end of the war, the North Korean landscape was charred by napalm, farmland had flooded, electrical outages were rampant, and countless cities, towns, and villages had been destroyed. Surviving North Korean citizens took shelter in underground caves that had been constructed by the Japanese during World War II. Despite the widespread destruction, North Korea continued to hold its position along the 38th parallel.

A Heavy Toll

After the spring of 1951, the line between North and South Korea held firm with the enemies entrenched on either side. Neither side made significant advances across the divide for the next two years. Truce talks began on July 10, 1951, although the fighting continued with deadly airstrikes and skirmishes across the heavily defended divide.

By the time the truce talks reached a successful conclusion in 1953, the war had taken a heavy toll across the peninsula. Carpet-bombing—the method of methodically covering and destroying an area with bombs—had annihilated

U.S. bombers dropped tons of explosives in North Korea, such as these that destroyed warehouses and other facilities in the city of Wonsan in 1951.

much of the North. Southern cities also bore the scars of battle. Seoul had exchanged hands four times, and both North and South Korean forces had occupied it at different times. Homeless refugees were left with few resources in both states.

The loss of human life was profound. Close to 3 million Koreans died, around half of them civilians. China also suffered heavy casualties. The war killed about 37,000 UN troops, mainly Americans, and wounded about 100,000 more.

Each of the war's main forces committed shocking atrocities. Guerrilla fighters from the North were famously ruthless. UN and American soldiers who were captured often faced torture, execution, starvation, and other forms of abuse. South Koreans were similarly brutal in their handling of suspected communist sympathizers, who were frequently rounded up and killed.

In recent years, journalists have shed light on incidents of U.S. troops targeting civilians during the Korean War. The history of the town of No Gun Ri, for example, shows the horrors of the war for civilians. Even though many Koreans were forced from their homes throughout the war, U.S. troops were under orders to prevent all Korean civilians from traveling. In July 1950, as a group of refugees made their way through

The war forced thousands of Koreans from their homes. Many chose to immigrate to other countries, including the United States and China.

No Gun Ri, newly arrived U.S. troops massacred them. The United States feared the presence of guerrilla fighters disguised as civilians, which may have motivated the attack, although the U.S. military maintains that no official order to attack was given. Nonetheless, over the course of 3 days, between 100 and 300 refugees were killed. The tragedy at No Gun Ri was just one example of civilians who were defenseless in the grip of the fighting. Whether or not they were purposely targeted, about 1.6 million Korean civilians were killed during the war.

Armistice

The two-year stalemate leading up to the armistice, or cease-fire, was a sign of the uncompromising nature of both sides. In October 1951, the truce talks had been moved to the village of P'anmunjŏm, just north of the 38th parallel. This town became the site of prolonged negotiations as the fighting carried on across the border.

North and South Korea argued bitterly over the terms of peace, including the release of prisoners of war. According to the Geneva Convention of 1949, prisoners of war (POWs) were supposed to be immediately freed and returned to their home country when a war ended. This practice did not suit the South Koreans, who argued that many of the POWs they held were actually South Koreans who had served with North Korea against their will. Requiring the return of these soldiers would deny them true freedom. On the other hand, China and North Korea insisted on the return of all POWs, knowing that if they did not, many POWs would choose to stay in South Korea.

As they negotiated, each side agreed to provide a count of the prisoners of war in their custody. The UN forces reported that they held 20,700 Chinese soldiers and 95,531 North Koreans. The United States had 11,500 troops who were missing in action. Expecting this number to be reflected in the POW count, U.S. officials were shocked when North Korea declared they had detained only 3,190 Americans. The difference in numbers for South Korean soldiers were even more dramatic. About 88,000 were missing in action, but North Korea could only account for 7,142. Many of those unaccounted for likely died in battle, but suspicions about the execution of POWs by the North Koreans and Chinese seemed to be confirmed. About 15,000 soldiers, mostly South Koreans, are

South Korean guards are shown here taking Chinese soldiers, captured while fighting in North Korea in 1950, to their trial.

REPATRIATING REMAINS

Four neutral nations helped in the effort to repatriate POWs, or help them return to their home countries, after the Korean War. Sweden, Switzerland, Poland, and Czechoslovakia screened troops to determine their willingness to return to their home countries. India assisted by housing POWs during the process. The bulk of repatriation occurred between August 5 and September 6, 1953.

Missing U.S. soldiers and their remains are still a major point of tension between the United States and North Korea. Although 3,597 U.S. soldiers were repatriated in 1953 and 2,700 died in captivity, about 8,000 were still missing. Between 1990 and 1994, North Korea began returning the remains of American soldiers. From 1996 to 2005, the U.S. sent funding and teams of workers to help with the investigations and repatriation efforts in North Korea. This partnership ended abruptly in 2005 after disputes over North Korea's nuclear weapons program.

As of 2018, 7,675 American veterans of the Korean War were still unaccounted for. However, a June 2018 agreement between North Korean leader Kim Jong-Un and U.S. president Donald Trump led to the return of more remains for identification. Since the war, the repatriation of remains has been a requirement for other collaborations between the United States and North Korea.

to returning POWs, meaning he would manage an exact exchange of one POW from each side until all U.S. troops were returned. The remaining POWs held by UN forces would be screened and returned to North Korea and China if they wished, but they would not be forced to go against their will.

Political changes in 1953 led to a climate that was more conducive to peace talks. Joseph Stalin, the dictatorial leader of the Soviet Union who had encouraged the continuation of the war, died on March 5, 1953. In the United States, Dwight D. Eisenhower had recently been elected president. Eisenhower wanted to end the war, which had already cost the United States $67 billion and 36,000 lives.

In April, China agreed to the voluntary repatriation of POWs, meaning they would allow the prisoners they held to return home. As a sign of good will, both sides participated in an exchange of sick and wounded POWs. Finally, on July 27, 1953, an armistice was signed. This agreement called for a cease-fire and the formation of committees that would help bring home POWs. Though it ended the fighting, the armistice was not a peace treaty. To this day, a formal peace treaty has never been signed between North and South Korea.

believed to have died after capture by the Communist forces.

President Truman decided to pursue a "one for one" approach

DIVIDED FAMILIES

One result of the Korean War was the permanent separation of many Korean families. As the conflict raged, Koreans fled the chaos across the country or were drafted into opposing armies. By the end of the war, the strict boundary between North and South made it impossible for relatives on different sides of the border to contact each other.

The first government-approved reunion of North and South Korean families took place more than three decades after the war, in 1985, under Kim Il-Sung. Supervised meetings briefly connected parents and children, husbands and wives, sisters and brothers, and extended family members. There have been 21 such events during times when relations between North and South Korea have been relatively warm.

In August 2018, a new reunion was organized after a three-year break. Kim Jong-Un and South Korean president Moon Jae-In agreed to let 170 separated families spend 11 hours together over a three-day period. The majority of the individuals involved were in their 80s and 90s. During the emotional reunions, Koreans were able to share gifts, family photos, and memories. They were finally able to connect with loved ones they had not seen in 65 years—and likely never would again.

Reuniting relatives is a matter of urgency for aging members of both nations. Here, 92-year-old Lee Keum-seom embraces her 71-year-old son. He was four years old when he was separated from Lee.

Soldiers from North Korea and South Korea uneasily monitor each other at P'anmunjŏm. Both sides continuously patrol the line that separates the two countries, and U.S. troops are a constant presence on the South Korean side.

The DMZ

The people and landscape of Korea suffered terribly during the war. Both sides sought to reunify the peninsula as one nation, but in the end, the boundaries of North and South Korea remained largely unchanged. In fact, the border created by the armistice lies in roughly the same location as the 38th parallel. The area between the two nations is known as the demilitarized zone, or the DMZ.

The DMZ is defined by a central line that separates the two nations and is padded by 1.2 miles (2 km) of land on each side, making it about 2.4 miles (4 km) across. From the Han River in the west to the town of Kosong in the east, the border is about 150 miles (240 km) long. Despite its name, this area is far from demilitarized. The zone is heavily patrolled by armed guards; electric fences, barbed wire, and land mines threaten those who try to cross without permission. With constant vigilance, troops on both sides of the DMZ stay alert for invasions and ambushes, which have occurred periodically since the DMZ was created.

The heavily guarded village of P'anmunjŏm provides the only break in the ribbon of land between North and South Korea. This village is located directly on the demarcation line. Six blue UN conference huts straddle the line, and buildings on both sides are designated as peaceful places for meetings between officials. A thick band of concrete separates North from South. Since an attack in 1967, soldiers are generally forbidden to cross this line. This is the last Cold War border and the only spot on the peninsula where North and South Korean troops actively face off.

Since the end of the Korean War, the rest of the DMZ has become an overgrown buffer between the warring nations. Aside from the fact that the area is littered with more than 1 million land mines, it provides a relatively wild nature preserve for thousands of plants and animals. Made up of wetlands, forests, and estuaries, the zone is home to birds, fish, amphibians, reptiles, mammals, and more than 1,000 insect species. Several species of crane are notable residents, along with Asiatic black bears, lynxes, and possibly even tigers.

Many of the species that thrive in the former battleground of the DMZ are endangered in more developed areas of the peninsula. In a country still recovering from the environmental devastation of war, deforestation, and industrialization, the DMZ is a unique refuge. Ecologists are eager to protect the area should reunification of the country ever occur. It is ironic that one of the most dangerous and heavily guarded areas of the peninsula has become such an important sanctuary.

CHAPTER FOUR

A FAMILY OF LEADERS

Modern Korean history has been dominated by the Kim family name. Kim Il-Sung was hand-picked by the Soviet Union to lead North Korea as a Communist state. His charismatic personality and status as a war hero made him a popular and natural leader. Kim Il-Sung led North Korea out of the devastation of the Korean War, building up North Korea's industries and resources with support from the Soviet Union and China. Propaganda distributed throughout the country exaggerated his accomplishments even more and encouraged the people to idolize him as the "Eternal Father" of North Korea.

When Kim Il-Sung died in 1994, the country entered a period of mourning and uncertainty. Kim's son, Kim Jong Il, had been slowly taking political control toward the end of Kim Il-Sung's life. When Kim Jong Il took full power after his father's death, North Korea became the world's first communist monarchy, in which leadership passed from father to son. Although this was unusual for Communist states, it was consistent with Korea's long history of Confucian kingdoms and dynasties in which power passed through family lines.

Kim Jong-Un is the most recent leader in the Kim family. When he took over after his father's death in 2011, Kim Jong-Un inherited a legacy of isolationism, militarism, and the violent suppression of opposition. The biographies and personalities of all three leaders have been heavily manipulated by the state to create a culture of leader worship and loyalty. Judged from a distance, the harsh political actions of all three Kims are difficult to reconcile with their public image within North Korea as loving leaders.

Kim Il-Sung

The story of Kim Il-Sung's life makes

Kim Il-Sung's name reflects his calling as the "Sun of Korea." His first wife, Kim Jong Suk, was also a guerrilla fighter. Kim Jong Il grew up to inherit his father's dictatorship.

up an important part of the curriculum for schools across North Korea. Born near P'yŏngyang on April 15, 1912, Kim Il-Sung moved to Manchuria with his parents at a young age to avoid the terrors of the Japanese occupation. He attended school in China and joined the Communist Party. He fought among the Korean guerrilla fighters in Manchuria before fleeing to the

右きリーダーとして

Soviet Union.

In the Soviet Union, Kim Il-Sung was trained in the military and caught the attention of Joseph Stalin as a potential leader for Communist Korea. After Japan surrendered to the Soviets in 1945, Kim Il-Sung returned to Korea for the first time since his childhood. The Soviet Union supported his rise to power and helped him become the chairman of the Korean Workers' Party in 1949.

After two unsuccessful petitions to Stalin, Kim Il-Sung eventually received Soviet approval for his campaign to reunite the Korean peninsula by force in 1950. He led North Korea through the war as the state's premier. The armistice of 1953 ushered in a new era of reconstruction and state-building under the direction of the "Great Leader."

Throughout the 1950s and 1960s, North Korea surged ahead of South Korea in using its resources and reconstructing its economy. Soviet funding made it possible to rebuild the ruined cities of the North, renew agricultural production, and provide services to the North Korean people. As a working Communist nation, North Korean citizens were required to labor for the state. In return, they received health care, education, housing, and government-issued goods and food. Private farms were taken under state control in 1958 and combined into more than 3,000 cooperatives for feeding the people of North Korea.

This period of growth reinforced Kim Il-Sung's control over North Korea and encouraged the idolization of Kim as a leader. Kim also protected his position through the brutal repression and execution of rivals and critics. Kim's regime made it a priority to instill communist ideals throughout the country. Propaganda was everywhere. Public art, children's stories, patriotic songs, films, and all aspects of the education system promoted the idea that the North Korean people and leadership were supreme.

Propaganda simultaneously focused on exalting Kim Il-Sung and smearing North Korea's international foes, especially the United States and Japan. Koreans remembered the crimes and atrocities of the Americans and Japanese, and the North Korean state kept anti-imperialist sentiments

Kim Il-Sung's image is visible across North Korea in mosaics, murals, towering statues, and even a life-size wax figure. These propagandized images promote the view of Kim Il-Sung as a benevolent genius who worked selflessly for his people.

alive through exaggerated and one-sided narratives of the war. A combination of fear and respect ensured Kim Il-Sung's power as the leader who had saved Korea from "American dogs" and Japanese imperialists.

Juche Philosophy

After the war, North Korea's government policies echoed the isolationist priorities of the 19th century's Hermit Kingdom. Korea's recent history as an occupied country made the people eager to seek national independence. In addition, Kim Il-Sung likely believed it was necessary to isolate North Korea from foreign powers in order to preserve his firm grip on the country. North Korea's borders were closed, so its people could not judge the merits of their government and society against those of the larger world. Instead, they were spoon-fed myths of Kim Il-Sung's goodness and North Korea's superiority.

This strict isolationist policy was justified through the Juche philosophy introduced by Kim Il-Sung. Juche is a model of political, economic, and military independence. It emphasizes self-reliance and encourages active, universal participation in revolution and state-building. This model understandably appealed to citizens

THE DAY OF THE SUN

Kim Il-Sung's birthday on April 15, 1912, is an important day in the North Korean calendar. North Koreans view this day as the birth of their country, and they have reset the national clock so that 1912 is commonly known as year one. April 15 is celebrated throughout North Korea as "The Day of the Sun," a national holiday. North Korean children receive a rare bag of sweets, and citizens dress up to attend elaborate parades, military rallies, fireworks shows, and performances that honor their country's founder.

The significance of this day points to the strong cult of personality that has developed around Kim Il-Sung. A cult of personality arises when mass media and propaganda are used to promote an idealized figure. Images of Kim Il-Sung are found everywhere in North Korea. Stories of his bravery, wisdom, and greatness provide material for everything from nursery rhymes to popular songs and television programs. Children are taught to be like their leader, who supposedly began his anti-imperialist activities at the age of five. At least publicly, Kim Il-Sung is worshipped and revered as the father of the North Korean people.

who had been under the control of foreign powers for decades. North Koreans were eager to reclaim their national identity and determine the course of their own future.

The Juche philosophy is still a guiding force for North Korean politics. According to the DPRK's official website, "The Korean people value the independence of the country and nation and, under the pressure of imperialists and dominationists, have thoroughly implemented the principle of independence, self-reliance and self-defense, defending the country's sovereignty and dignity firmly."[8] The ideology is also known as Kimilsungism-Kimjongilism in North Korea today.

All citizens must work to make Juche a reality. In theory, the self-sufficiency of the people is used in service to the greater good of the state. Juche is directed by one great leader who unites the efforts of the people and steers the state toward success and independence.

Introducing Juche in the 1950s was a strategic action by Kim Il-Sung to tighten his grip on the country. It was used to silence criticism within the state and to pull North Korea away from the Soviet Union's influence. Discontent in the Soviet Union threatened to weaken Kim Il-Sung's status as an infallible leader if it spread to North Korea, so withdrawing from the Soviet Union offered Kim Il-Sung a way to maintain control.

The Juche Tower in P'yŏngyang is one of the highest monuments in the world. It was commissioned to celebrate Kim Il-Sung's 70th birthday in 1982.

Economic Trouble

Kim Il-Sung introduced Juche into North Korean policies, but it was not always successful. North Korea still relied heavily on economic aid from its Communist allies, China and the Soviet Union. As these sources of aid began to dry up, North Korea's economy faltered. In the 1970s, a stagnating economy began to erode postwar gains.

Excessive military spending in the 1960s had sapped many of the resources that could have been used to support agricultural and industrial growth. Government spending was used to develop large-scale industry at the expense of being able to supply everyday goods that people needed. These financial decisions, combined with a rise in population, caused food shortages to be a problem.

Kim Il-Sung continued to centralize control of North Korea by introducing a new constitution in 1972. The Socialist Constitution of the Democratic People's Republic of Korea changed his position from premier to president of the DPRK. It also made Juche the country's official ideology, which cemented Kim Il-Sung's authority even more. However, this move came with a cost. Under this policy of isolation that limited foreign involvement in North Korea's economy, only China and the Soviet Union were allowed in, and a recession took hold.

In the 1980s, Communism outside of North Korea began to disintegrate.

By the 1990s, North Korea's allies started to distance themselves from the floundering country. The Soviet Union fell in 1991, marking the end of the economic aid that had kept North Korea afloat. China also took a step back from North Korea and established new and friendly ties with South Korea. The loss of foreign aid and protection would test the strength of North Korea as a young country.

The Eternal Leader and the Dear Leader

North Korea reached out to the United States and South Korea in an unprecedented way after the fall of the Soviet Union, although its ultimate goals were unclear. Both North Korea and South Korea joined the United Nations in 1991. This new development led to two agreements between the rival nations. North Korea had launched at least two terrorist attacks against South Korea in the 1980s, but now they pledged to work toward reconciliation. The two countries also signed a joint agreement that would ban nuclear weapons from the peninsula. There was continued controversy over the use of nuclear weapons, however, and the measures did not survive. North Korea again cut ties with South Korea in 1993.

In 1994, Kim Il-Sung began negotiations with U.S. president Bill Clinton. The goal was for North Korea to abolish its nuclear development program in exchange for U.S. assistance in installing more electricity throughout the country. This exchange established a pattern of relations with the United States, and since then, North Korea has used its nuclear development program as a bargaining chip in international negotiations.

As part of the 1994 negotiations, South Korean president Kim Young-Sam planned to attend an unprecedented meeting in North Korea. However, the day before Kim Young-Sam was scheduled to arrive, Kim Il-Sung died of a heart attack at age 82, and the negotiations did not go forward. Instead, North Korea hurtled into a period of mass, public grieving while the outside world speculated about whether the country could survive.

The defector Hyeonseo Lee remembered the effects of Kim Il-Sung's death in her hometown:

Several thousand students and teachers joined in the sobbing and the wailing. The grief seemed to be getting more extreme by the hour. A kind of hysteria was spreading across the city. Our schooling stopped. The steel and lumber mills, the factories, shops and markets closed. Every citizen had to participate in daily mass events to demonstrate their inconsolable sorrow …

After the mourning period, as I'd feared might happen, punishment awaited those who had shed too few tears. On the day classes resumed the entire student body gathered in front of the school to hurl criticism and abuse at a girl accused of faking her tears … Many adults across the city were similarly accused and the Bowibu [state security department] made a spate of arrests. It wasn't long before notices began appearing, giving the time and place for clusters of public executions.[9]

As the nation's citizens expressed their grief, whether genuine or faked, they also wondered what would happen next. Starting in the 1980s, Kim Il-Sung had begun to promote his son in the government and mark him as his successor. Kim Jong Il had been the Supreme Commander of the Korean People's Army since 1991, even though he had never served in the army. Despite his prominent leadership roles and the name "Dear Leader," Kim Jong Il was a shadowy figure. Aside from his artistic tendencies, the public knew very little about him. In general, he lacked his father's charisma and authority, and he very rarely spoke in public. Many onlookers from outside North Korea doubted that he would be able to control the country as his father had.

For unknown reasons, Kim Jong Il waited three years before taking charge of North Korea. Instead of replacing his father as president, Kim Jong Il became the head of the

Dramatic scenes of grief-stricken North Koreans characterized 10 days of national mourning after the death of the "Great Leader." Kim Il-Sung's embalmed body has been on display in P'yŏngyang since his funeral.

Korean Workers' Party and the country's "Supreme Leader." Kim Il-Sung was named the "Eternal Leader" and standing president of North Korea through an amendment to the constitution in 1998. As the Lonely Planet travel guide to Korea cheekily pointed out, Kim Il-Sung is "the world's only dead head of state."[10]

Famine in North Korea

In the three years between his father's death and his own assumption of power, Kim Jong Il had steadily built his base of support. During those years, however, North Korea's people suffered terribly. Food shortages had plagued the country since 1993, and a number of factors came together to create a widespread famine in the mid-1990s. For one thing, North Korea is a mountainous country with limited areas of good farmland, and it was not producing enough food to feed its growing population. Meanwhile, food supplies coming from other countries had stopped.

Natural disasters added to the problem in 1994 and 1995, when massive flooding destroyed more than a million tons of grain, took out 85 percent of Korea's power generating capacity, and damaged other infrastructure. The government cut daily rations from 1 pound (450 g) of food per day to just over a quarter of a pound (128 g). Between 1994 and 1998, it is estimated that

KIM JONG IL, THE FILM FANATIC

Kim Jong Il had a reputation outside North Korea as an eccentric leader. He had a passion for international cinema and collected more than 20,000 films. He also installed a movie theater in each of his residences. Kim Jong Il was dissatisfied with the quality of North Korean films, which relied over and over on the same basic plots centered on North Korean ideology and nationalism. In the 1970s, he looked for ways to enhance the artistry of North Korean films and be included in international film festivals.

A famous South Korean actress named Choi Eun-Hee was abducted under orders from Kim Jong Il in 1978. Her husband, film director Shin Sang Ok, was also brought to North Korea. The two were detained separately in North Korea for several years and "reeducated" in the communist ideology. Eventually, they were reunited, and Kim Jong Il gave them access to a large film studio, artistic license, and an unlimited filmmaking budget. Although North Korean film was traditionally a propaganda tool, Choi and Shin were allowed to expand to other genres. The duo created seven films under Kim Jong Il's patronage, and they were permitted to attend European film festivals escorted by bodyguards. In 1986, they were able to escape to an American embassy in Vienna, Austria. Their stories from being in Kim Jong Il's inner circle shed light on his erratic behavior and personality, as well as his disregard for the rights and wishes of others.

up to 3.5 million North Koreans died of starvation.

In *North Korea Undercover*, British journalist John Sweeney provided a firsthand testimony from a defector named Ji Seong-ho. Ji's desperation for food led him to steal coal from a train in an attempt to sell it. In the process, he fell onto the train tracks and lost his hand and leg. Like many other defectors, extreme hunger pushed Ji Seong-ho to escape from North Korea. This is his account of the famine's effects:

I think I lost my mind from dizziness, sleep deprivation and hunger. My grandmother and my neighbors died of starvation. It wasn't just where I lived. When you went into the cities, train stations, markets and alleyways, you found lots of dead bodies. I do not know the exact number but countless people died. Countless.[11]

Choi Eun-Hee (left) and her husband Shin Sang Ok (right) eventually escaped their North Korean captors and moved to the United States.

This period of economic hardship and food insecurity ended many of the nation's strict communist practices. People turned to market-based activities even though they were prohibited by communism and the North Korean constitution. In their struggle for survival, citizens traded whatever services they could provide or goods they could scrape together. Some gathered and sold sticks for firewood, others hawked household items, and families with more resources made simple broths or soups to sell. The entire country was gripped by the famine. Even citizens of P'yŏngyang, the privileged capital city, felt the effects of hardship. Journalists Daniel Tudor and James Pearson commented on the famine's impact in their 2015 book, *North Korea Confidential*:

The state refers to this calamity as the "Arduous March," the name of a legendary wartime campaign said to have been waged by Kim Il Sung as

North Korea's famine in the 1990s resulted from the mismanagement of national funds, the end of Soviet subsidies, and the effects of natural disasters that wiped out crops.

a young guerrilla fighter. It may be seen as darkly ironic that the North Korean state's greatest failure—and the one that effectively ended the socialist economic system that Kim Il Sung "marched" to build—has been dressed up in such terms.[12]

Kim Jong Il publicly denied the famine's existence. Instead of taking a cooperative attitude in order to receive foreign aid, he continued to toy with international deals, talks, and boasts about nuclear weapons. Western countries debated about whether to offer help or to refuse assistance because North Korea was a nuclear threat. Eventually, Japan, South Korea, the United States, and international agencies such as the World Food Programme came in with emergency food and medical care.

Songun Policy

Kim Jong Il's preoccupation with nuclear weapons was related to the national Songun policy. This policy promotes the idea of "military first." It prioritizes military spending and the development of armed forces and sophisticated weapons. Although Kim Il-Sung developed this idea, Kim Jong Il channeled a great deal of energy and resources into its application.

The Korean People's Army (KPA) of North Korea is composed of four branches: Ground Forces, Navy, Air

DESPERATE TIMES

During the famine, North Koreans were forced to get creative in finding food sources. Many accounts tell of people eating grass or making soups with flour and water. In the book *Ask a North Korean*, a defector named Mina Yoon recalled her struggle to find food in the countryside:

It was tough to find anything edible. When you went out to the mountains, plenty of people were already competing to dig out edible herbs. Farmland was another battlefield for digging out the rice roots remaining in the soil.

These rice roots would be ground into powder and made into porridge, or maybe some rice noodles. Though not as good as rice itself, the roots still contain some useful nutrients ...

If you remove the thick, tough outer layer of pine trees, there's another layer before you get to the white flesh of the tree. There's a thin brown film between the outer skin and the white core. People peel off that thin film and pound it into fine powder. Then they add a couple tablespoons of flour to make a cake. So, basically, it is a cake made with tree bark and it actually tasted quite decent.[1]

1.   Quoted in Daniel Tudor, *Ask a North Korean: Defectors Talk About Their Lives Inside the World's Most Secretive Nation.* North Clarendon, VT: Tuttle Publishing, 2017, pp. 151–52.

Force, and civil security forces. It is the fourth largest military in the world. Military service is mandatory for all citizens, so more than 1 million of the country's 25 million citizens are on active duty in the military, and as many as 6 million trained troops are in the reserves.

Entering the military at 17 years old, North Korean men serve for a minimum of 10 years, and women are required to serve until age 23. Young people who attend university enter the military after finishing their education. Some complete a reduced term depending on their field of study. Although serving in the military is regarded as a patriotic duty and privilege, many service members endure severe hardships. For example, soldiers can serve up to six years before they are granted their first home visit. They also face the same problems of hunger and poverty as their non-military neighbors. Between 20 and 22 percent of North Korea's national budget is devoted to the military. However, not much of the money goes toward providing food and accommodations for soldiers. Under the Songun policy, the money is spent on developing military technology and weapons. In addition to its substantial manpower and weapons arsenal, North Korea also has large fleets of planes, helicopters, tanks, submarines, ships, rockets, armored vehicles, and missile launchers.

Kim Jong Il and his Songun policies gained momentum in the 1990s and 2000s as the country developed nuclear programs. In 2003, Kim Jong Il backed out of the United Nations Nuclear Nonproliferation Treaty and instead brazenly worked to increase the country's nuclear capabilities. In October 2006 and again in May 2009, Kim Jong Il oversaw the first public nuclear tests in North Korea. The UN has condemned North Korea's military goals by instituting sanctions, or restrictions on trade, against the country. These are designed to stop North Korea's nuclear growth by cutting off sources of money and materials.

Despite these sanctions, Kim Jong Il forged ahead with his Songun mission. His stated goal was to protect North Korea from foreign invasions by amassing weapons and building a formidable army. Within North Korea, citizens still fear foreign attacks. Beginning with Kim Il-Sung's regime, North Koreans have been taught to see foreign invasions as a constant threat. In defector Je Son Lee's view, most North Koreans support nuclear armament as a necessary safety measure:

The brutality of the Japanese and U.S. military are depicted in textbooks. North Koreans read such textbooks from their kindergarten years.

Pictures and graffiti of Japanese and American soldiers committing acts of violence are painted on the buildings of kindergartens, schools, and offices in North Korea. If you grow up being brainwashed and exposed to such an environment from kindergarten onwards, how would you feel? North Koreans grow up realizing the importance of protecting their own country.

This leads to the justification of the possession of nuclear weapons. The North Korean government doesn't teach its people about the negative side of the nuclear program. So, ordinary North Koreans have no way of finding out how dangerous nuclear weapons can be.[13]

Though North Koreans themselves may have accepted Kim Jong Il's seeming obsession with military might, governments around the world severely disapproved. They saw Kim Jong Il's narrow-minded focus on military strength as a sign that he was a negligent leader. Even as the military grew under his direction, the North Korean people continued to suffer from hunger and health crises.

During his early days in power, Kim had appeared more open to international cooperation than his father, but his friendly overtures to other nations were unpredictable and unreliable. In the end, only his commitment to militarism seemed to matter.

The Brilliant Comrade: Kim Jong-Un

Concerns over Kim Jong Il's health came to light in 2008 when he appeared to suffer a stroke. In 2009, he began introducing a successor into P'yŏngyang's official circles, just as his father had done before him. Kim Jong-Un is the youngest of Kim Jong Il's three sons. Although his age is not confirmed, he was likely born in 1984. As a child, he attended school in Switzerland before returning to Korea and the Kim Il-Sung National War College in P'yŏngyang.

Kim Jong Il appointed Kim Jong-Un to a number of positions within the government. He joined the National Defense Commission and was elevated to the rank of four-star general, although it is unlikely that he served in the military. In P'yŏngyang, Kim Jong-Un became known as the "Brilliant Comrade."

On December 17, 2011, Kim Jong Il suffered a fatal heart attack while on a train trip touring military sites. He was 70 years old. Kim Jong Il's death was publicly announced to the Korean people two days later, and the nation was plunged into an official period of mourning for the second time in its history. Kim Jong-Un escorted his father's coffin in a public funeral procession in which the Korean people hysterically wept and wailed, just as they had done for Kim Il-Sung. Kim Jong Il's embalmed body lies near his father's at the Kumsusan Palace of the Sun.

Kim Jong-Un swiftly took the country's reins after his father's funeral, becoming North Korea's new, and fearsome, Supreme Leader. He immediately launched a government purge to replace the top tier of P'yŏngyang officials. The officials were not simply fired: South Korean intelligence suggests that more than 300 officials were executed during Kim Jong-Un's first 5 years in power.

One of the first confirmed executions occurred in December 2013. Kim Jong-Un denounced his uncle Jang Song-Thaek, who was a high-ranking official and had advised Kim Jong-Un in his early days in power. Kim expelled him from the Communist Party as a traitor and ordered his death. This brutal treatment of his own family raised fears about the ruthlessness of Korea's newest dictator. It also drove a wedge between North Korea and China, where Jang had formed close ties. It seemed Kim Jong-Un would stop at nothing to ensure his power.

While Kim Il-Sung's rule was characterized by the introduction of Juche and Kim Jong Il promoted Songun, Kim Jong-Un introduced the byungjin strategy, which focuses on the parallel

development of the military and the economy. His first years in office were marked by rapid advances in military growth; however, the economy lagged behind.

Between 2013 and 2017, Kim Jong-Un oversaw six increasingly sophisticated nuclear tests. He has boasted that North Korea possesses a hydrogen bomb—a particularly powerful nuclear weapon—as well as a vast supply of other nuclear weapons. His menacing claims have served to isolate North Korea more than ever.

Under Kim Jong-Un's direction, the North Korean military has rigorously tested missiles and rockets. By 2017, North Korea possessed long-range ballistic missiles that were advanced enough to reach the continental United States.

THE DEATH OF KIM JONG-NAM

On February 13, 2017, a man named Kim Jong-Nam was killed with a powerful chemical nerve agent at a busy airport in Malaysia. Kim Jong-Nam was Kim Jong-Un's half-brother, the eldest son of Kim Jong Il. Kim Jong-Nam had left North Korea with his family in 2001 and had not returned since his brother took power. Before Kim Jong Il's death, Kim Jong-Nam had spoken out against the idea of a third generation of the Kim family taking power in North Korea. In 2012, he also openly criticized his brother's qualities as a leader.

Kim Jong-Nam's death is believed to be the result of an assassination operation ordered by Kim Jong-Un and carried out by North Korean agents. Like the execution of his uncle, this murder exposed the hostile and extreme measures Kim Jong-Un was willing to use to suppress opposition, even within his own family. It also drew attention to North Korea's arsenal of chemical weapons. The chemical used in the attack is highly lethal and internationally banned. With this assassination, Kim Jong-Un sent a clear message: He would not tolerate dissenters, and he had the ability to eliminate them if he so chose.

In his address to the Korean people on January 1, 2017, it was clear that he was using North Korea's nuclear program to intimidate his rivals and promote an image of national and personal strength. However, Kim Jong-Un's approach seemed to have grown more cooperative by 2018, as indicated by landmark meetings with South Korea and the United States.

CHAPTER FIVE

MAKING HEADLINES

Despite repeated withdrawals from the international sphere, North Korea consistently captures the attention of the outside world. In the 21st century, it is difficult for Westerners to understand or even imagine living in a country where the government restricts nearly every aspect of life.

The ongoing humanitarian crisis in North Korea also attracts international attention. Kim Jong-Un's regime has been intent on securing the country's borders and controlling information, operating a police state that rigidly defines acceptable behavior and severely punishes those who break the rules. There are many reports of human rights abuses in North Korea, mainly from the personal accounts of defectors who risked their lives to escape.

From the outside, North Korea appears to be a living time capsule of the Cold War era, lacking the technological innovations of the modern era and excluded from current trends in the global community. However, North Korea is on the cutting edge when it comes to military weapons. The country has devoted its scant resources to building a vast arsenal of nuclear, chemical, and perhaps even biological weapons. This dogged pursuit has given them a prominent place on the world map and ensures the close attention of foreign powers.

Life in North Korea

North Korea today is divided into nine provinces, each with a regional government. The details of daily life vary depending on the city or province. For example, life in the capital city of P'yŏngyang is remarkably different from life in rural areas. P'yŏngyang is a showcase for the nation's ideology and is the center of tourism. About 12 percent of the population lives in P'yŏngyang. Most foreign

This satellite image dramatically illustrates the differences between North Korea and its neighbors. Aside from a few areas, North Korea is submerged in darkness at night. Electrical blackouts are still a common problem.

visitors receive a highly structured and limited view of North Korea, composed mainly of the landmarks, museums, and cultural attractions of P'yŏngyang. As the capital, P'yŏngyang is also the center of political activity. The leaders of the Workers' Party of Korea live and work there.

The Constitution of North Korea was created in 1948 and replaced in 1972, and the new constitution has been revised and amended periodically. The rights supposedly guaranteed by the constitution include freedom of speech, freedom of religion, freedom of assembly, the right to vote, the right to universal and free health care and education, and the right to limited property. However, these rights and activities are only allowed if they are in service to the state. In actual practice, the activities of North Koreans are strictly controlled by the government, which decides what is best for the state. For example, citizens who criticize the government or assemble in groups of more than three people without permission can be sent to prison camps. Communist countries are traditionally anti-religion, and in North Korea, state-approved worship is centered on the Kim family. Voting is a right and requirement for all North Koreans over age 17, but all political candidates run unopposed, so votes are merely symbolic. Health care, food, housing, and quality education are meant to be provided by the state, but the nation's struggling economy has meant that these services are only guaranteed to the top tier of state officials.

The constitution recognizes four different categories of citizens: peasants, soldiers, workers, and working intellectuals. Society is further divided by a system called *songbun*. This ranking system establishes a social hierarchy that is a reminder of Korea's ancient past. Songbun is a hereditary system based on loyalty to the state and the Communist Party. For example, having a grandfather who cooperated with Japanese colonialists

is enough to land a person in the bottom, "hostile" tier of songbun. On the other hand, being directly related to anti-Japanese guerrilla fighters can put someone in the "core" tier. The core tier receives privileges such as larger rations, better access to education, and potentially a residence in P'yŏngyang. Recently, songbun has become less influential as communist practices and their associated perks have waned.

The government still keeps a tight grip on many of the actions of ordinary citizens, down to what clothing and hairstyles are considered acceptable. Traditionally, women have been required to wear skirts and dresses, though now they may wear pants as long as they extend beyond the knee. Women cannot dye their hair and must keep it in one of 15 approved styles. Men are also required to choose one of 15 short hairstyles. Students from elementary school to university are required to wear school uniforms. According to recent defectors, fashion trends from South Korea are beginning to appear, and regulations are less strictly enforced. Still, all adults must wear a party pin with an image of Kim Il-Sung when they go out in public.

Travel between cities and villages is restricted to people with government permits. Although a small minority of North Koreans have access to cell phones and computers, they can only use the state's private networks, which are strictly censored. Contact with foreigners and foreign media is rare. All foreign visitors are screened by the North Korean government and generally only come to North Korea through state-approved tour groups, humanitarian organizations that supply aid workers, or business contracts. Foreign journalists are occasionally invited to state-sponsored events such as the Arirang Mass Games. Most tour groups do not accept applicants from the United States, and the U.S. State Department has issued a "Do Not Travel" advisory for its citizens. When all visitors arrive, regardless of their nationality or purpose for travel, they are assigned North Korean "handlers" who accompany them everywhere. In this way, the state controls what

North Koreans can be fined or imprisoned for failing to wear their party pin or not displaying state-issued portraits of Kim Il-Sung and Kim Jong Il in their homes.

sights visitors see, what they photograph, and who they talk to. This also prevents most North Koreans from communicating with outsiders.

Human Rights Abuses

The forcible oppression of the North Korean people has fueled the success of the Kim family dynasty. The epic scale of human rights violations threatens people at every level of North Korean society, from the highest government officials to the lowest rural peasants. In addition to daily suppression and censorship, the state stages public executions and operates prison camps to control its people. Defector Jang Jin-Sung argued that propaganda and oppression are so effective because "people in North Korea have no concept of basic human rights. They do not know what they should be entitled to. They have nothing to fight for."[14]

In the face of international criticism about its history of human rights abuses, the North Korean government recently responded to defend its actions. An article in the official state newspaper asked, "Is there any country on the earth like the DPRK where the people fully enjoy political freedom and democratic rights as masters of the society?" It went on to assert, "Nothing can cover up the brilliant reality of the DPRK where the people enjoy genuine rights at the highest level as real masters of the state and society and no one on earth

can block the bright path ahead of the DPRK."[15]

Despite these remarks, insights provided by defectors and humanitarian aid organizations within the state tell a different story. North Korea's political prisons have been a fixture since Kim Il-Sung ruled. They grew even more under Kim Jong Il and Kim Jong-Un's power. Offenses as slight as expressing dissatisfaction with the Kim family or simply being related to a defector can land a North Korean in prison. Ji-min Kang, who defected in 2005, said,

Even North Korean children know that North Koreans can be taken to political detention camps and that if they are taken to one, they will not be able to return to the outside world again. Of course, there is no legal process, such as a trial. They are simply taken away by a truck in the night and nobody knows where they have gone.

They do not notify their family members or relatives, and if family members go and protest, the authorities threaten them and don't reveal anything about the whereabouts of their loved one.

Anyway, the most important thing is that they are guilty. This is a horrendous contravention of the

THE GLAMOROUS CITY

In North Korea, 97 percent of roads are unpaved. Only 11 in 1,000 North Koreans own a car. Poverty, hunger, illness, and lack of heat, electricity, and clean water all plague North Koreans outside the capital city of P'yŏngyang. There, however, the streets are pristine, residents have access to reliable utilities, and there are even places for entertainment. Ji-min Kang, a North Korean defector, recalled the special appeal of the capital:

> North Korea is a small country—you can reach anywhere by airplane within an hour. But countless people die there without visiting Pyongyang even once. That's because the government does not allow its people to move from one place to another without the relevant travel documents and a good reason for travel. It is very difficult to do so except on business trips or for family events. Entry into Pyongyang is strictly controlled due to the security of the Kim family and the dense military presence there. So Pyongyang is seen as a dream city that everyone wants to visit: The only city in North Korea that has a theme park and zoo; the only place you can enjoy culture, the arts, and sports. It's even home to the country's only bowling club![1]

1. Quoted in Daniel Tudor, *Ask a North Korean: Defectors Talk About Their Lives Inside the World's Most Secretive Nation*. North Clarendon, VT: Tuttle Publishing, 2017, p. 93.

constitutional values of North Korea. Both South and North have freedom of expression. But North Korea has no freedom after expression.[16]

Satellite images taken over North Korea reveal vast complexes of prison camps. One of these camps sprawls across an area three times larger than Washington, D.C. It is estimated that 120,000 North Koreans are currently imprisoned in places that have been compared to the German concentration camps of World War II. About 400,000 are believed to have died in the camps already. Political prisoners are forced to work even as they are starved, tortured, and sexually assaulted, and sometimes they are executed.

Defectors

The system of collective punishment for family members is meant to discourage defections and actions

P'yŏngyang was leveled during the Korean War. The government had to start from scratch to construct the many landmarks and monuments in this city of 3 million residents.

against the state. If an individual defects, several generations of the family, and even extended relatives, can be sent to prison camps. Jang Jin-Sung was a propaganda poet in Kim Jong Il's regime when he defected in 2004. Reflecting on the repercussions of his decision to flee, he said, "If you want to protect the people you love, you keep your mouth shut and you carry on. If you choose to break the rules, you must be prepared to have blood on your hands."[17]

Over the years, defectors have chosen to escape despite the potential consequences. During the famine years, many left out of desperation as their friends and neighbors starved around them. Others have left for political reasons or to seek greater freedom and opportunity. Since the end of the Korean War, more than 30,000 North Koreans have successfully defected to South Korea.

A DIFFICULT JOURNEY

Hyeonseo Lee was 17 when she escaped North Korea in 1997. She lived in China in hiding for 10 years before she could make her way to South Korea by way of Laos. In her memoir, *The Girl with Seven Names*, she described the difficult decision to leave her country, the struggle to adjust to a new life in South Korea, and her complicated feelings about her home country:

> *I grew up knowing almost nothing of the outside world except as it was perceived through the lens of the regime. And when I left, I discovered only gradually that my country is a byword, everywhere, for evil. But I did not know this years ago, when my identity was forming. I thought life in North Korea was normal. Its customs and rulers became strange only with time and distance. Thus I must say that North Korea is my country. I love it. But I want it to become good. My country is my family and the many good people I knew there. So how could I not be a patriot?*[1]

1. Hyeonseo Lee, *The Girl with Seven Names: Escape from North Korea*. London, England: William Collins, 2015, p. xiii.

Hyeonseo Lee has written a memoir, given a TED talk, and met with world leaders to tell her story of defecting and advocating for loved ones still in North Korea.

The most common escape route is across the Yalu River into China. Many wait until winter so they can cross the ice on the river. Defectors risk being shot, killed, or captured by North Korean border guards during their crossing. Even after reaching China, they are in great danger. North Koreans caught traveling illegally in China are often sent back to their home country, where they are imprisoned or executed. Some successful defectors choose to live under the radar in China as they save money. Others continue on to Mongolia or Laos with the help of paid guides or charity groups. From there, they can travel to South Korea.

Once defectors arrive in South Korea, they are questioned and detained by the government. During this period, they are also provided with training to prepare them for life in a capitalist society. When they have completed their training, the South Korean government provides

defectors with housing and a living allowance as they adjust to their new life. The process can be daunting and lonely for North Koreans who have left behind friends and family and often find it difficult to fit into South Korean society.

A small minority of defectors have left by crossing the dangerous territory of the DMZ, others have gone by water, and some high-profile North Koreans have defected while traveling abroad. Regardless of what route they have chosen, all defectors have risked their lives to leave. Their stories and experiences help the outside world understand the realities of life in North Korea.

North Korea and the United States

Ever since the Korean War began, North Korea has considered the United States one of its greatest enemies, and anti-American sentiment is a main theme in the nation's

On September 23, 2017, an anti-U.S. rally and military parade was held in P'yŏngyang. It was meant to showcase the power and organization of the North Korean people and their readiness to rise up against attackers.

propaganda. On the other side of the coin, the United States has been quick to vilify North Korea. As the historian Bruce Cumings has observed, "Judging from our media, North Korea is the country every American loves to hate."[18]

In his 2002 State of the Union Address, U.S. president George W. Bush grouped the dangers and crimes of North Korea together with those of Iran and Iraq: "North Korea is a regime arming with missiles and weapons of mass destruction, while starving its citizens," he said. Bush went on to denounce the pursuit of weapons among these countries, saying, "States like these, and their terrorist allies, constitute an axis of evil, arming to threaten the peace of the world. By seeking weapons of mass destruction, these regimes pose

great strength and patience, but if it is forced to defend itself and its allies, we will have no choice but to totally destroy North Korea."[20]

Despite this threatening and aggressive rhetoric, the year 2018 actually brought warmer relations between the United States and North Korea. On June 12, 2018, Trump and Kim Jong-Un were the first leaders in the history of the two countries to meet face-to-face. By the end of their five-hour talk, North Korea had pledged to work toward complete denuclearization. The United States in turn agreed to end its joint military exercises with South Korea.

A few months later, during his 2019 New Year address, Kim Jong-Un told the people of North Korea, "I am ready to meet the US president again anytime, and will make efforts to obtain without fail results which can be welcomed by the international community." He followed up this offer with a threat:

a grave and growing danger."[19]

President Donald Trump echoed these sentiments in his 2017 speech to the UN. Trump began by criticizing the negligence and violence of Kim Jong-Un: "No one has shown more contempt for other nations and for the wellbeing of their own people than the depraved regime in North Korea. It is responsible for the starvation deaths of millions of North Koreans, and for the imprisonment, torture, killing, and oppression of countless more." Trump ended his criticism with a direct threat: "The United States has

But if the United States does not keep the promise it made in the eyes of the world, and out of miscalculation of our people's patience, it attempts to unilaterally enforce something upon us and persists in imposing sanctions and pressure against our Republic, we may be compelled to find a new way for defending the sovereignty of the country and the supreme interests of the state and for achieving peace and stability of the Korean peninsula.[21]

A second summit between Trump and Kim Jong-Un, in February 2019, did not go as well as the first. Trump abruptly cut the talks short when Kim Jong-Un did not agree to U.S. demands for North Korea's complete denuclearization in return for lifting economic sanctions against the country. In the wake of the failed meeting, satellite images suggested North Korea was beginning to prepare launching sites in the country, perhaps to resume missile testing. As always, the future of the relationship between North Korea and America is tense and uncertain.

The Korean Peninsula

Some progress has been made in relations with South Korea. In February 2018, North and South Korean athletes marched under a common Korean flag at the Winter Olympics in Pyeongchang, South Korea. In an unprecedented move, Kim Jong-Un's sister, Kim Yo-Jong, also attended the Olympics. It was the first time a Kim family member had visited South Korea since 1950. Kim Yo-Jong delivered a handwritten letter from her brother inviting the South Korean president to visit.

On April 27, 2018, Kim Jong-Un and Moon Jae-In met at P'anmunjŏm for

In a symbolic gesture, the leaders of North and South Korea shook hands across their shared border in P'anmunjŏm.

historic peace talks. The discussions focused on denuclearization and the armistice between the two countries that had been put in place in 1953. Both sides showed interest in adopting a formal peace treaty that would finally bring the Korean conflict to an end.

In his 2019 New Year address, Kim Jong-Un also discussed a potential partnership with South Korea and the long-standing goal of unification. In his characteristic style, he balanced his peaceful gestures with another threat:

It is our steadfast will to eradicate military hostility between north and south and make the Korean peninsula a durable and lasting peace zone … We will never tolerate the interference and intervention of outside forces who stand in the way of national reconciliation, unity and reunification with the design to subordinate inter-Korean relations to their tastes and interests.[22]

The relationship between North and South Korea has been on shaky footing since the Korean War. Its history is a combination of friendly overtures and highly charged attacks. Moving forward, the resolve of the two nations to diligently work toward peace will undoubtedly be tested.

WHO ARE NORTH KOREANS?

North Korea frequently makes its way into Western news headlines, but the country's past and present still remain a mystery to outsiders. The country's continued existence seems to defy reason. As author Victor Cha observed, "The regime remains intact despite famine, global economic sanctions, a collapsed economy, and almost complete isolation from the rest of the world."[23]

So who are North Koreans? It is easy to label the country's leaders as eccentric, its policies as backward, or its people as brainwashed. In order to better understand North Korea, however, it is necessary to dig deeper. The answer is complex, sometimes contradictory, and always colored by the long history of Korea from its existence as a unified and ancient nation until today.

The Road Forward

Understanding North Korea from the outside requires a comprehensive view of history. For countries such as the United States and Japan, this means recognizing the destructive role of foreign occupation and war on the peninsula. As historian Bruce Cumings suggested, "In human rights circles, the easiest thing has always been to look one way and condemn the communists, while ignoring the reprehensible behavior of our allies."[24]

A long view of history shows North Korea's steadfast efforts to be independent and prepared for self-defense. The nation's build-up of nuclear weapons has its roots in the decades when the peninsula suffered under the thumb of the Japanese and in the three years when North Koreans lived underground as American bombs rained down on their homes and villages. To truly appreciate and connect with North Koreans, these countries will have to acknowledge the long and painful legacies of occupation and the Korean War.

The cult of personality surrounding Kim Il-Sung and Kim Jong Il is tied to the historical and political roots of North Korea.

As South Korea, the United States, and other countries attempt to develop friendlier relationships with North Korea, they will also need to determine how to support defectors and confront the human rights abuses that are rampant under the Kim regime. Hopefully, the common goal of peace will guide these efforts on all sides.

"Let Morning Shine"

In September 2018, North Korea held its first Arirang Mass Games in five years. These enormous athletic displays are a marvel of precision, coordination, training, and dedication. A defector named Mina Yoon described the primary goal of the spectacle: "The mass games in North Korea were designed to highlight the legitimacy and consistency of the regime by showcasing its strong spirit of community for the outside world to see ... The government wanted its people to believe that North Korea was the most strongly united country in the world."[25]

In the five years that had passed since the last Mass Games, a great deal had changed in North Korea, and the country continues to evolve. A market economy has slowly infiltrated the communist society, introducing not only new sources of food and goods, but also media. According to defectors, it is now common for North Koreans to secretly buy thumb drives loaded with South Korean and Western television shows, radio broadcasts, and music.

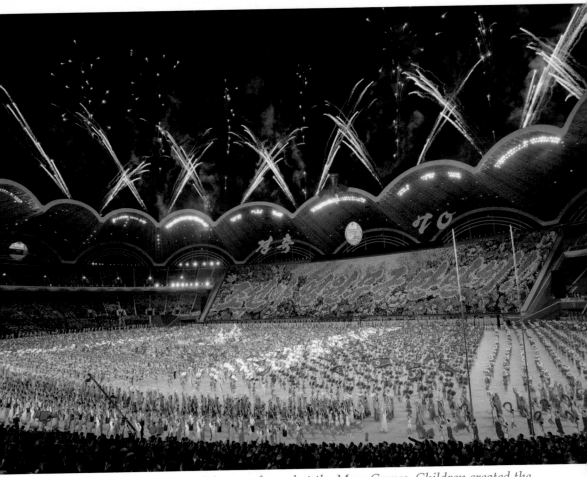

Gymnasts, dancers, and musicians performed at the Mass Games. Children created the pixelated background images by holding large, colored cards.

As new ideas, information, and views of the outside world come to North Korea, its culture is likely to evolve. Already, cell phones and the internet are changing the way people connect and communicate in North Korea, even if they are limited to private state networks. While the state is eager to put on a display of absolute unity in the service of the regime, the reality of everyday life is changing. In North Korea, the land of morning calm, a new sun may be rising.

Notes

Introduction:
The Secret State

1. Quoted in Liz Sonneborn, *North Korea*. New York, NY: Children's Press, 2014, p. 64.

Chapter One:
Kingdoms and Dynasties

2. Peter H. Lee, ed., *Sourcebook of Korean Civilization: Volume 1: From Early Times to the Sixteenth Century*. New York, NY: Columbia University Press, 1993, p. 125.

Chapter Two:
The World at War

3. "Treaty of Portsmouth," The World War I Document Archive, last updated May 20, 2009. wwi.lib.byu.edu/index.php/Treaty_of_Portsmouth.

4. Quoted in Hildi Kang, *Under the Black Umbrella: Voices from Colonial Korea*. Ithaca, NY: Cornell University Press, 2001, pp. 17–18.

5. "The Cairo Declaration," Wilson Center Digital Archive Collection, accessed on January 7, 2019. digitalarchive.wilsoncenter.org/document/122101.

6. Quoted in Michael Fry, "National Geographic, Korea, and the 38th Parallel," *National Geographic*, August 4, 2013. news.nationalgeographic.com/news/2013/08/130805-korean-war-dmz-armistice-38-parallel-geography/.

Chapter Three:
The Korean War

7. Bruce Cumings, *The Korean War: A History*. New York, NY: Modern Library, 2010, pp. 22–23.

Chapter Four:
A Family of Leaders

8. "Juche Ideology," Democratic People's Republic of Korea, accessed on January 7, 2019. www.korea-dpr.com/juche_ideology.html.

9. Hyeonseo Lee, *The Girl with Seven Names: Escape from North Korea*. London, England: William Collins, 2015, pp. 72–73.

10. Simon Richmond, *Korea*. Oakland, CA: Lonely Planet, 2010, p. 355.

11. Quoted in John Sweeney, *North Korea Undercover: Inside the World's Most Secret State*. New York, NY: Pegasus Books, 2015, p. 233.

12. Daniel Tudor and James Pearson, *North Korea Confidential: Private Markets, Fashion Trends, Prison Camps, Dissenters and Defectors*. North Clarendon, VT: Tuttle Publishing, 2015, p. 18.

13. Quoted in Daniel Tudor, *Ask a North Korean: Defectors Talk About Their Lives Inside the World's Most Secretive Nation*. North Clarendon, VT: Tuttle Publishing, 2017, p. 85.

Chapter Five:
Making Headlines

14. Quoted in Enjoli Liston, "Jang Jin-Sung: 'If Anyone Thinks North Korea Is Opening Up, They Are Mistaken,'" *Guardian*, May 7, 2014. www.theguardian.com/world/2014/may/07/north-korea-defector-jang-jin-sung-pyongyang-book-dear-leader.

15. "Open Questionnaire to Human Rights Schemers Issued," *Rodong Sinmun*, January 1, 2019. www.rodong.rep.kp/en/index.php?strPageID=SF01_02_01&newsID=2019-01-01-0019.

16. Quoted in Tudor, *Ask a North Korean*, p. 49.

17. Quoted in Liston, "Jang Jin-Sung: 'If Anyone Thinks North Korea Is Opening Up, They Are Mistaken.'"

18. Bruce Cumings, *North Korea: Another Country*. New York, NY: The New Press, 2003, p. vii.

19. "Text of President Bush's 2002 State of the Union Address," *Washington Post*, January 29, 2002. www.washingtonpost.com/wp-srv/onpolitics/transcripts/sou012902.htm.

20. "Remarks by President Trump to the 72nd Session of the United Nations General Assembly," The White House, September 19, 2017. www.whitehouse.gov/briefings-statements/remarks-president-trump-72nd-session-united-nations-general-assembly/.

21. "Kim Jong Un's 2019 New Year Address," NCNK, January 1, 2019. www. ncnk.org/resources/publications/kimjongun_2019_newyearaddress. pdf/file_view.

22. "Kim Jong Un's 2019 New Year Address," NCNK.

Epilogue:
Who Are North Koreans?

23. Victor Cha, *The Impossible State: North Korea, Past and Future*. New York, NY: Ecco, 2012, p. 7.

24. Cumings, *North Korea: Another Country*, p. xiii.

25. Quoted in Tudor, *Ask a North Korean*, p. 248.

For More Information

Books

Lee, Hyeonseo. *The Girl with Seven Names: Escape from North Korea*. London, England: William Collins, 2015.
   This heartfelt memoir provides a firsthand account of one defector's harrowing experience of living in and escaping from North Korea.

Sonneborn, Liz. *North Korea*. New York, NY: Children's Press, 2014.
   A chronicle of North Korea's history, this book also explores the people and culture of the secret state with the help of clear text and illuminating photographs.

Tudor, Daniel. *Ask a North Korean: Defectors Talk About Their Lives Inside the World's Most Secretive Nation*. North Clarendon, VT: Tuttle Publishing, 2017.
   This collection of interviews with defectors records their answers to a wide range of simple and complex questions about life in North Korea.

Tudor, Daniel, and James Pearson. *North Korea Confidential: Private Markets, Fashion Trends, Prison Camps, Dissenters and Defectors*. North Clarendon, VT: Tuttle Publishing, 2015.
   This exploration of life in the DPRK offers hope for the future and debunks many of the popular myths that still color the perception North Korea by the outside world.

Websites

The Committee for Human Rights in North Korea
www.hrnk.org
   The HRNK website offers updates on its strategies and efforts to end human rights violations in North Korea.

Daily NK
www.dailynk.com
   By using internal contacts and reports from defectors, Daily NK provides up-to-date information from within North Korea.

Democratic People's Republic of Korea
www.korea-dpr.com
   This official webpage for the DPRK government presents explanations of history and policies from a distinctly North Korean perspective.

NK News
www.nknews.org
   NK News provides news stories, interviews with defectors, and analyses of current events related to North Korea from its headquarters in Seoul, South Korea.

North Korean Economy Watch
www.nkeconwatch.com
   This website keeps a close eye on ups and downs in the North Korean economy and their social repercussions.

Rodong Sinmun
www.rodong.rep.kp
   The articles in *Rodong Sinmun*, the official newspaper of the Workers' Party in North Korea, give international readers a sample of DPRK propaganda.

The Wilson Center: Conversations with Kim Il Sung
digitalarchive.wilsoncenter.org/collection/138/conversations-with-kim-il-sung
   This vast archive presents transcriptions and primary documents that record Kim Il-Sung's communications with Communist allies and others.

Index

A

Arduous March, 69
Arirang Mass Games, 80, 93–94
As I Saw It (Rusk), 41
assassinations, 32, 76

B

Bell of King Sŏngdŏk, 21
Bird Bishop, Isabella, 36–37
Bronze Age, 13–15
B-29 planes, 45
Buddhism, 17, 20–22, 24–27
Bush, George W., 86

C

Cairo Conference, 40
celadon pottery, 24
cell phones, 79, 94
Cha, Victor, 91
China, 9–10, 13, 16–18, 20, 24, 27,
    29–33, 40–41, 43–45, 47–48, 50, 52,
    64, 74, 84
Chosŏn dynasty, 6, 27, 29–30, 32, 36
Chosŏn muntcha. See Hangul
civil service exams, 20, 27
Clinton, Bill, 64
comfort women, 39
Communist Party, 41–43, 58, 74, 79
Confucianism, 17, 20, 24, 26–27, 37
Cumings, Bruce, 44, 86, 91

D

defectors, 12, 65, 68, 72–73, 77, 79,
    81–85, 93
demilitarized zone (DMZ), 56, 85
Democratic People's Republic of
    Korea (DPRK), 8, 42, 62, 64, 81
dolmens, 14–15

E

Eisenhower, Dwight D., 52
executions, 29, 47, 50, 59, 65, 74, 76,
    81–82, 84

F

farms, 10, 14–15, 39, 45, 59, 67, 72
Fatherland Liberation War. *See*
    Korean War
films, 35, 59, 68
food, 10, 13–14, 33, 39, 45, 59, 64,
    67–69, 71–72, 79, 93

G

Ganghwa, Treaty of, 30
*Great Dharani Sutra of Immaculate
    and Pure Light, The*, 22
guerrillas, 35, 39, 41, 47, 49, 58, 71,
    79

H

Hangul, 27, 37
human rights, 77, 81, 91, 93
Hwanin, 14

Hwanung, 14–15, 17

I

Iron Age, 15
Iryeon, 17
isolationism, 8, 30, 57, 61

J

Jang Jin-Sung, 81, 83
Jang Song-Thaek, 74
Japan, 6, 10, 13, 27, 29–33, 34–41,
   45, 59, 61, 71, 73, 79, 91
Japanese occupation, 10, 35, 38–41,
   43, 58
Jikji, 25
Ji Seong-ho, 68
Juche, 61–62, 64, 74

K

Kang, Ji-min, 81–82
Kaya Confederacy, 18
Khan, Kublai, 26
Kim Il-Sung, 7, 10, 12, 39, 41–42, 44,
   53, 57–67, 71, 73–74, 79–81, 93
Kim Jong Il, 7, 12, 16, 57–58, 65,
   67–68, 71, 73–74, 76, 80–81, 93
Kim Jong-Nam, 76
Kim Jong-Un, 7, 12, 52–53, 57,
   74–77, 81, 87–88, 90
Kim Yo-Jong, 88
Kim Young-Sam, 65
Koguryŏ, 17–20, 23
Kojong (emperor of Korea), 30,
   32–33, 35
Korea and Her Neighbors (Bird
   Bishop), 36
Korean People's Army (KPA), 43,
   65, 71
Korean War, 7, 10, 12, 43, 45, 47,
   52–53, 56–57, 83, 85, 90–91

Korean War, The (Cumings), 44
Korean Workers' Party, 59, 67
Koryŏ dynasty, 6, 23–27

L

Lee, Hyeonseo, 65, 84
Lee, Je Son, 73

M

MacArthur, Douglas, 42
Manchuria, 13–14, 18, 33, 39, 58
Mao Zedong, 44
Mongols, 25–27
Moon Jae-In, 53, 90
mourning, 57, 65–66, 74
Mumun pottery, 14

N

napalm, 45
Neo-Confucianism, 27, 29
No Gun Ri, 47, 49
Nokchin, 26
nuclear weapons, 64, 71, 73, 75, 91

O

Old Chosŏn, 13–17

P

Paekche, 17–18, 23
Paleolithic Period, 13
P'anmunjŏm, 49, 54, 56, 89–90
Parhae, 20
Pearson, James, 69
police states, 77
Portsmouth, Treaty of, 33–34
poverty, 12, 72
prisoners of war (POWs), 49–50, 52
prisons, 79, 81–83
propaganda, 10–11, 57, 59, 62, 68,
   81, 83, 86

P'yŏngyang, 9, 15, 19, 58, 63, 66, 69, 74, 77–79, 82–83, 86

R

refugees, 47, 49
Rhee, Syngman, 42
Roosevelt, Franklin, 40
Roosevelt, Theodore, 33–34
Rusk, Dean, 41
Russia, 9–10, 13, 20, 30, 33–34, 45. *See also* Soviet Union
Russo-Japanese War, 33

S

Samguk sagi, 26
Samguk yusa (Iryeon), 17, 26
Sejong (king of Korea), 27
Seoul, 40–42, 44–45
Shimonoseki, Treaty of, 33
Silhak, 29
Silla, 6, 17–18, 20–24, 26
Sino-Japanese War, 30–31, 33, 36
social classes, 17, 20, 22, 26–27, 29, 37
Socialist Constitution of the Democratic People's Republic of Korea, 64
songbun, 79
Songun, 71–74
South Korea, 8, 10, 13, 15, 20, 22, 25, 27, 42–45, 47, 49–54, 56, 59, 64–65, 71, 74, 76, 79, 83–85, 87–90, 93
Soviet Union, 10, 12, 41–45, 52, 57–59, 62, 64

Sunjong (emperor of Korea), 35
Sweeney, John, 68

T

Tangun, 6, 15–17
38th parallel, 6, 41–42, 44–45, 49, 56
Three Kingdoms period, 6, 17–18, 20, 22
Tonghak Uprising, 31
Tripitaka Koreana, 25
Truman, Harry S., 44–45, 52
Trump, Donald, 52, 87–88
Tudor, Daniel, 69
2018 Winter Olympics, 86

U

United Nations (UN), 37, 42, 44, 47, 50, 52, 56, 64, 73, 85
United States, 10–11, 29–30, 40–45, 49–50, 52, 59, 64–65, 69, 71, 75–76, 80, 85–87, 91, 93

W

Wang Kŏn, 6, 22–23
Wilson, Woodrow, 35–36
woodblock printing, 22, 25
World War I, 35
World War II, 10, 37, 39–41, 45, 82

Y

Yalu River, 20, 84
Yi Sŏng-gye, 6, 27
Yi Sun-shin, 28–29
Yoon, Mina, 72, 93

Picture Credits

About the Author

Eleanor Bradshaw lives in New York with an ever-expanding collection of books. She is the author of several nonfiction titles for young readers. In addition to writing, she enjoys researching and finding overlooked details that bring the past to life. She spends her spare time traveling, cooking, and enjoying nature.